Under the Haw

The time is the 1840s
the Great Famine. Eily, Michael and
Peggy are left alone, but they set out on a
long and challenging journey to find the
grand-aunts they know only from their
mother's stories.
*A moving story of resourcefulness and
adventure, impossible to forget.*

The Author
This is a first novel from Marita Conlon-McKenna.
She has also written stories for the very young and
a book on the first communion experience. Marita
lives in Dublin with her husband
and four children.

'...she has created a sublime story
...enthralling...'

CLODAGH CORCORAN *The Irish Times*

Now available
the sequel to this book
WILDFLOWER GIRL

For my daughter
Amanda
'the little mother'

Acknowledgements
A special note of thanks for their
support and encouragement to the
following: my husband James, my
mother and father Mary and Patrick
Conlon, my Aunt Eleanor (Murphy),
Brigid Brady, Pat Donlon, Anne
O'Connell and the Tyrone Guthrie
Centre, Annaghmakerrig.

WINNER OF THE
INTERNATIONAL READING ASSOCIATION
AWARD 1991

Some comments on winning this award:

'A cause for pride and celebration. . .
A remarkable achievement'

Dr Pat Donlon – Director of The National Library of Ireland

'the achievement represents a benchmark
in the development
of children's writing in this country'

Eamonn Murtagh – President, Reading Association of Ireland

'for the writer . . . and Irish publishers in general
it represents a great breakthrough'

*Dr Vincent Greaney – Educationalist
and board member of The International Reading Association*

First published 1990 by The O'Brien Press Ltd.,
20 Victoria Road, Dublin 6, Ireland.

British Library Cataloguing in Publication Data
Conlon-McKenna, Marita
Under the hawthorn tree.
I. Title
823.914

ISBN 0-86278-206-6

10 9 8 7

Typeset at the O'Brien Press
Book design: Michael O'Brien
Editing: Ide ní Laoghaire
Illustrations: Donald Teskey
Separations : The City Office Dublin
Printing: The Guernsey Press Co. Ltd.

The O'Brien Press receives assistance from
The Arts Council/An Chomhairle Ealaíon.

Contents

UNDER THE HAWTHORN TREE

Marita Conlon-McKenna

Illustrated by Donald Teskey

THE O'BRIEN PRESS
DUBLIN

CHAPTER 1

Hunger

 THE AIR FELT COLD and damp as Eily stirred in her bed and tried to pull a bit more of the blanket up to her shoulders. Her little sister Peggy moved against her. Peggy was snoring again. She always did when she had a cold.

The fire was nearly out. The hot ash made a soft glow in the gloom of the cottage.

Mother was crooning quietly to the baby. Bridget's eyes were closed and her soft face looked paler than ever as she lay wrapped in Mother's shawl, her little fist clinging to a piece of the long chestnut-coloured hair.

Bridget was ill – they all knew it. Underneath the wrapped shawl her body was too thin, her skin white and either too hot or too cold to the touch. Mother held her all day and all night as if trying to will some of her strength into the little one so loved.

Eily could feel tears at the back of her eyes. Sometimes she thought that maybe this was all a dream and soon she would wake up and laugh at it, but the hunger pain in her tummy and the sadness in her heart were enough to know that it was real. She closed her eyes and remembered.

It was hard to believe that it was only a little over a year ago, and they sitting in the old school room, when Tim O'Kelly had run in to get his brother John and told them all to 'Make a run home quick to help with lifting the spuds as a pestilence had fallen on the place and they were rotting in the ground.'

They all waited for the master to get his stick and shout at Tim: Away out of it, you fool, to disturb the learning, but were surprised when he shut his book and told them to make haste and 'Mind, no dawdling,' and 'Away home to give a hand.' They all ran so fast that their breath caught in their throats, half afraid of what they would find at home.

Eily remembered. Father was sitting on the stone wall, his head in his hands. Mother was kneeling in the field, her hands and apron covered in mud as she pulled the potatoes from the ground, and all around the air heavy with a smell – that smell, rotting, horrible, up your nose, in your mouth. The smell of badness and disease.

Across the valley the men cursed and the women prayed to God to save them. Field after field of potatoes had died and rotted in the ground. The crop, their food-crop was gone. All the children stared – eyes large and frightened, for even they knew that now the hunger would come.

Eily snuggled up against Peggy's back and soon felt warmer. She was drowsy and finally drifted back to sleep.

'Eily! Eily! Are you getting up?' whispered Peggy.

The girls began to stretch and after a while they threw off the blankets. Eily went over to the fire and put a sod of turf on the embers. The basket was nearly empty. That was a job for Michael.

Both girls went outside. The early morning sun was shining. The grass was damp with dew. They didn't delay as it was chilly in their shifts. Back in the cottage, Mother was still asleep and little Bridget dozed against her.

'Is there something to eat?'

'Oh, Michael, easy known you're up,' jeered Eily.

'Go on, Eily, look, have a look,' he pleaded.

'Away outside with you and wash that grime off your face and we'll see then.'

The sunlight peered in through the open cottage door. The place is dusty and dirty, thought Eily.

The baby coughed and woke. Eily took her and sat in the fireside chair as Mother busied herself. There were three greyish leftover spuds. Mother sliced them and poured out a drink of skimmed milk from the large jug. It was little enough. No one spoke. They ate in silence, each with their own thoughts.

Michael began to talk ... to ask for ... but changed his mind. Time had taught him a lesson.

The first few times he had asked for more, his father or mother had lifted the wooden spoon and brought it down on the palm of his hand. Later, his pleas had been met by a sadness in his father's eyes and his mother bursting into tears. This he could not take on top of the pinches and squeezing of his two sisters. Things were better left unsaid.

By midday the situation had improved. There was heat in the sun and a warm breeze blowing.

Michael went up the road to his friend Pat and together they would walk the mile to the bog to see if they could get a fill for the basket.

Bridget's breathing was rattly, but she slept. Mother, encouraged, took the shifts and a few dirty clothes to wash and then spread them outside to dry. She shook the blankets and laid them across the stone wall.

Peggy's long brown hair was unplaited. It hung lank and greasy. Mother bent her over as she poured water from the bucket on the hair and scrubbed at her scalp. The cries from Peggy were nothing to what followed when Mother produced the fine comb and began to pull it through the length and tangles, peering each time to see if any lice or nits were in it. Eily laughed, knowing that since she had had her turn only two weeks before, she would escape today.

Later, Mother despatched the two of them up the lane to Mary Kate Conway for a bit of goose grease – if she had it – to rub on Bridget's chest. Mary Kate had a gift for healing and always helped those who were sick or in trouble.

Her cottage was surrounded by a thick hedge in order to provide a bit of privacy for those who needed to visit her.

The old lady was sitting on a stool outside in the sunshine.

'Well, if it isn't the two best little girls in the world,' joked Mary Kate. 'What can I do for you, pets?'

'Mother needs some goose grease for the baby,' pleaded Eily.

'The poor, poor child,' murmured Mary Kate. 'What a time to come into the world.' She got up from her stool and beckoned to the girls to follow her. Peggy lagged behind, clutching at Eily's dress. She had heard stories about the old lady and was a bit afraid of her.

The cottage was dark and smelly. Mary Kate hobbled over to the old wooden dresser. It was filled with jars and bottles. She mumbled to herself as she lifted down different jars and opened the lids to peep at the contents. Finally, sniffing what she wanted, she handed it down to Eily.

'Mind you tell your mother I want my jar back when she is finished.'

'Will it make Bridget better?' Eily was amazed at the bravery of little seven-year-old Peggy's question.

Mary Kate frowned. 'I don't know, pet. There is so much sickness at the moment – strange sickness

– I do my best.'

With that, Mary Kate began to head back out towards the sunlight. Just outside the door she put her hand into the pocket of her apron and produced an apple. A dirty old apple. She gave it a polish. The girls tried not to look, but with a flourish she handed it to Peggy.

Peggy's eyes were round and wide. Eily blinked.

'Many thanks … we couldn't take it from you … thank you, but it wouldn't be fair,' Eily began.

'As green and hard as the hobs of hell,' laughed Mary Kate, throwing back her head to display her toothless gums. 'Shure, I can't eat it.'

The girls smiled and Peggy carried the apple like a precious jewel safely home to be shared by all.

That night they had the yellow meal cooked with some melted lard and a few wild spring onions Mother had found to hide the flavour. The apple was quartered and savoured, though there was no denying its crisp hardness and sharp taste.

'It is two weeks since your father went to work on the roads, and still no word from him,' began Mother. Eily knew her mother was worried, between Bridget's illness and the sack of the old yellow meal in the corner getting smaller and smaller by the day.

'I don't know what we'll all come to or how we'll manage,' Mother continued, shaking her head. 'There is even talk of the big house being closed up and the master and his family moving back to England for good.'

Michael, sensing the near despair in her voice, piped up: 'I've got some good news. Listen, Ma, just listen.'

Sometimes it was hard to believe that he was only a boy of nine, with his thick black curly hair like his father and the soft kind blue eyes of his mother. He hated to see her sad.

'Pat and I were up on the bog – we went a bit further than usual and we found a part that isn't all cut away yet. Pat's father is going up there tomorrow with him and will cut it and lay it and he says if this wind and drying continues we can have some for our place once we collect it and carry it ourselves. Isn't that grand?'

Mother smiled. 'Dan Collins is a good man, there's no doubt.'

She settled herself into the chair and relaxed a bit. Eily knelt down near her and Peggy sat in her lap.

'Tell us about when you were a girl – go on, please,' they all begged.

'Are ye not all fed up with my old stories,' she chided.

'Never,' assured Michael.

'Well, then,' she began. 'Mary Ellen, that was my mother and your grandmother, what Eily's called after, lived with her two sisters Nano and Lena ...'

There was nothing like a story before bedtime.

CHAPTER 2

Under the Hawthorn Tree

 THE BREEZE CONTINUED. It was great drying weather. Dan Collins had sent a message to say he would take them to the bog that morning. Peggy kept hopping from one foot to the other with excitement. Since the hunger and sickness had come, the children spent most of their time hanging around the cottage. Mother wanted them near her. From their door the O'Driscolls could see the curling smoke from each cottage chimney that made up their small homeland of Duneen. It was a beautiful place. There were plenty of good neighbours, but nowadays there was very little visiting. Each family tried to hide its shame at having so little. Anyway, not many had the energy or the heart for singing, dancing and storytelling any more.

But today was different – Eily, Michael and

Peggy were going to the bog. They waved goodbye to Mother, who looked tense and pale. Baby Bridget was still very sick. She slept most of the time and cried only when Mother put her down.

They each carried a basket for the turf. Also there was a can of cool water and some potato skins and a crust of dry bread to keep the hunger at bay.

Pat and his father were waiting for them. Dan Collins was a big man, with curly blond hair, and his eyes seemed to twinkle when he was in a good mood. He spent most of his time outdoors and always seemed to know where wild berries or mushrooms grew. Moses, his old donkey, stood with the empty creels tied to his back.

'You bold young straps, holding us up on such a fine day,' joked Dan as he put the empty baskets on top of the donkey. 'Run on ahead and Moses and I will follow in our own good time.' The donkey was old and slow and would not be rushed.

The children had plenty of time to play and cod-act as they gathered the dry turf into neat piles. Peggy busied herself picking wild cowslips for Mother.

At last Dan arrived and they began to load the baskets with as much as they could carry, which wasn't too much. Old Moses was able for only a half-load nowadays.

In no time they were all hot and thirsty. They sat down and gulped the cool water and ate what they had. Dan had a sup of tea and a potato cake, and then he helped them all in turn to carry their baskets as Pat guided and steadied Moses.

The journey home was long and exhausting. The fields seemed stonier and their arms and shoulders and backs ached. They had to stop and rest often. A few times, Peggy sat down on the ground and said she couldn't walk any further, and began to sob. Dan Collins joked her and told her that if old Moses with his bad leg could do it surely a young pony like herself could manage it.

It took an age before they reached the Collins's cottage. There they said farewell. The children found the last half mile almost endless. Michael's hands were bleeding as he tried to keep a grip on the heaviest basket. It was dusk by the time they reached home.

The big basket would sit by the fire, but the rest was emptied at the side of the cottage. It made only a small pile. They couldn't help but remember the large pile you could stand on, almost the height of the cottage, that their father would normally gather when times were good.

They pushed in the door. Mother was dozing with Bridget in the chair near the fire. She looked tired and they could tell she had been crying.

Quiet as mice, they reheated some leftover oatmeal and water. They were all tired out, and glad to fall into bed. With arms and shoulders aching, they scarcely had time to notice the normal rumbling hunger pains that came before sleep.

At some time during the night they became aware of their mother's sobs and of Bridget coughing and trying to breathe. Michael came and lay down in the bed beside the girls. They held hands and prayed – every prayer they had ever learned.

'God help us, please help us, God,' they whispered.

No one slept. It was the early hours of the morning before the coughing stopped. Then there was a sudden silence. Mother was kissing the baby's face and each little finger one by one.

'God let the sun come up soon and let this terrible night end,' the children begged.

Suddenly they became aware of their mother's silence. They got up and went over to her. Large tears slid down her cheeks.

'She's gone. My own little darling is gone.'

Peggy started to cry. 'I want Bridget back,' she

wailed. 'I want her.'

'It's all right, pet,' assured Mother. 'She was too weak to stay in this hard world any longer. Look at her. Isn't she a grand little girl, now she's at rest.'

The baby lay still, as if she were just dozing. Mother told them to kiss her, and one by one they kissed the soft cheek and forehead of Bridget, the little sister they hardly knew.

Mother seemed strangely calm and made them go back to bed. 'At first light, Michael, you must run to Dan Collins and ask him to get Father Doyle. I'll just sit and mind my darling girl for a little while yet.'

Later, Michael set off, his face pale and his eyes red-rimmed. The chill of the early morning made him shiver as he pulled his light jacket around him.

Mother had heated some water and with a cloth she gently washed Bridget, and brushed and brushed the soft blond curls. Eily pulled the old wooden chest from under Mother and Father's bed. As instructed, she opened it. There wasn't that much in it, so she soon found the lace christening robe which her great-grandmother had made. The lace was yellow and old. It was only ten months since Bridget had worn the robe before, but her little body was so thin and wasted it still fitted her.

Dressed in it she looked like a little pale angel, though Eily couldn't help but remember a porcelain French doll she had seen in a shop window in the town once. It stood stiff in a white lace dress with a starched petticoat and long curling real hair. How she had wanted to hold and have that doll. Now she felt the same longing, but much worse. She ached to hold Bridget and never let her go.

Michael came home. They all had a sup of milk and tidied themselves and the cottage as best they could. Dan Collins would get the priest. Father Doyle was a nice man – he and Father were very friendly and sometimes he would drop in for a chat and a bit of company. Father used to say that being a priest was grand, but it was a lonely life.

Mid-morning they were all surprised when Dan Collins and his wife Kitty arrived. Kitty ran straight to Mother and kissed her. Their eyes were full of tears and unspoken words.

'Margaret, we are so sorry. Poor little Bridget,' whispered Kitty.

Dan Collins cleared his throat and shifted uneasily. 'There is more bad news, God spare us. Father Doyle is gone down with the sickness himself and will not be able to bury the wee lassie. Already in the village a few have died of the sickness – Seamus

Fadden, the coffin maker, being one – so there are no proper funerals ... ' He stopped.

Mother let out a high wailing cry. 'What will become of us, what are we to do?' The air hung heavy.

'We'll bury her decently in her own place,' said Dan.

The three children stared at Mother, waiting for her reply. She nodded her head silently.

'Under the hawthorn tree in the back field,' she whispered. 'The children always played there and its blossom will shelter her now.'

Dan motioned to Michael and they left the cottage and disappeared up to the field carrying a spade.

'We've no coffin,' said Mother hoarsely.

Kitty looked around the cottage and begged Eily to help her. Eily cleared her throat. 'What about using grandmother's wooden chest?'

Kitty and Eily pulled it out from under the old bed and lifted it onto the blanket. Mother walked over and nodded silently. Kitty began to take out the family treasures and lay them to one side.

Kitty and Mother started to get everything ready. Eily and Peggy, sensing they were not wanted, ran outside and pulled bluebells and wild flowers. They sucked in deep breaths of air to try and calm their hearts.

Dan came back down the field and went inside. In a few minutes the three adults emerged, Kitty holding Mother's arm and Dan carrying the carved wooden chest.

A light breeze blew and the blossom bowed and waved in welcome. There was a clear blue sky. A family of bluetits sat on the branch of the tree, helping to keep vigil.

Dan and Kitty led them in the prayers and they all remembered the words of Jesus, 'Suffer the little children to come unto me'. They prayed too that they would 'meet again in Paradise'.

Eily and Michael gently placed the flowers beside the chest. Peggy clung to Mother as huge sobs racked her body. Mother stroked her hair. They all sang a favourite hymn of Father Doyle's, then Kitty led them back to the house. She had brought some tea and made a mug for the adults. She made Mother sit down near the fire as she warmed some leftover potato cakes.

For the next few days, Mother stayed in her shift with the shawl wrapped around her, and barely bothered to do anything. Eily and Michael fetched the water, swept out the cottage and searched for food. They wished that Father would come back. Eily was scared. How long would it last?

CHAPTER 3

Nothing to Eat

A FEW DAYS LATER, Mother called them all together. She had built up the fire. She was dressed and her hair was pinned up with two combs. She had folded up her beautiful handworked lace shawl and grey knitted wedding gown with its matching lace collar and set them on the bed. Her Mother had made them for her, for that special June day when she had married John O'Driscoll many years before.

'Eily, share out the potato skins, then sit down.' They all had a drink and a bite to eat. Mother took up the brush and began to brush Peggy's long dark hair.

Then she slipped off her shift and put on a cream dress. 'Eily, Michael and Peggy, I have to go into the village today, because there's nothing left to eat. Bridget is gone. I have buried one child and I'll not let anything happen the rest of you. We must have food,' she said.

'But, Mother,' began Eily, 'you've no money ... oh no, not your dress and shawl, it's all you've left.'

'Listen, pet, what good is a dress and a shawl hidden away under the bed? I know they won't bring much, but maybe Patsy Murphy will trade me enough for a bag of meal and some oats or something. With every day we are all getting weaker and losing our strength. We must eat or we'll get sick. Do you think I can't see Peggy and the eyes shining out of her head and her arms and legs like sticks? And Michael, my little man, who can hardly lift the basket of turf and hasn't the strength to walk the few miles to the river to try and catch a bit of fish? And Eily, my darling girl, who is worn out with the worry of it all? Now, listen. You must keep the fire going and get some water in. You are all to stay indoors. Dan Collins told me that the sickness is everywhere and that people are out walking the roads. I will be as fast as I can, but you must keep the door on the latch.'

Eily begged, 'Please, Mother, let me go with you.'

Mother shook her head and insisted they stay. She put a few things in her basket and pulled on her shawl. Outside it was a beautiful warm morning. The fields were covered in daisies and the hedgerows were laden with woodbine and honeysuckle. It was tempting to stay outside and play, but they dared not disobey Mother. They waved goodbye.

Peggy was cross and cranky and bored. Michael invented games and tried to think of things to distract her, but Eily still had to resort to raising the wooden spoon twice. Peggy lay down on the bed sulking, and angry with Eily.

Suddenly they became aware of footsteps coming down the laneway. Could she be back so soon? Eily was about to rush out and help with the bag of meal when she realised that there were two voices outside. The children stayed still and silent.

'For the love of God, let a poor woman and her son in for a sit down and a sup of water,' whined the voice. They were standing just outside. 'We've walked for miles. We're tired and sore and thirsty.

A little help is all we need.'

Eily made to go towards the door, but Michael stopped her.

'Remember what Mother said,' he hissed. 'Don't answer.'

The strangers were tapping on the door. Quickly Michael moved the turf basket and the chair in front of it. The two girls sat on the ·bed, scared. What if they guessed there were only children in the house?

'Did you hear us?' The woman raised her voice. 'We need a bit of help.' When there was no reply, the woman began to curse. She picked up two pieces of turf and flung them at the door.

'There could be pickings inside,' said the son.

Eily and Michael and Peggy stared at each other, all terrified out of their wits, wondering what would happen when the strangers pushed in the door.

Suddenly Michael got an idea. 'Oh, thank God for someone coming along,' he moaned. 'We need help. Oh, for the love of God, run to the well and bring us a bucket of water. My sister is burning up with the fever and my throat and head feel they are on fire.'

Eily put a hand over Peggy's mouth to stop her

from giggling or saying something. The two voices outside the door whispered to each other.

'We buried my little sister last week,' continued Michael in a high quavering voice, 'and half the village is dying of the fever. For the love of God...'

The woman raised her voice. She had moved away from the door. 'We meant you no harm and God spare ye for we cannot stop. Come on, son, away from this place of sickness.' The two gathered up their bundle of rags and set off down the lane.

Once the children were sure the danger was past they hugged each other.

'Oh, Michael, what a funny brother you are,' joked Eily. 'How did you think of it? And yet you saved us all.' Michael blushed pink even to the tips of his ears. 'People will pay money to come and see you act. You'll be a player, and famous too,' added Eily.

With all the excitement, Peggy's humour improved and she ran around the cottage making up songs about her brave brother.

The sky had begun to darken and the sun was going down when they heard another knock at the door. They all froze and could almost hear the pounding of each other's hearts.

'It's me, children, it's Mother.'

Quick as a flash, they opened the door and flung themselves at her, part in welcome and part in relief.

'Wait, wait, you young scamps, don't knock me over. Let me get my breath back,' begged Mother. She had a few small parcels in her arms and she looked exhausted. Her hair hung loose around her face.

'Mother, your combs – your beautiful combs, they're gone too,' cried Eily.

'Your father always said he preferred my hair long and loose and free with the sun and the breeze through it. Well, now he'll have his wish,' said Mother, trying to smile.

'What did you get? What did you get?' asked Peggy, full of curiosity about what was in the parcels.

Mother put them up on the table and slowly opened each one. In times gone by the children would have paid no heed to Mother and her purchases from the village and would have kept on playing in the fields. But now their very lives depended on what was in those packages.

The largest was a bag of oatmeal. Then there was

a bag with a few pounds of greyish-looking spuds, then a tub of lard, a few screws of salt, and lastly a small hard piece of dried beef. It wasn't much.

'There is a large sack of yellow meal too,' added Mother, sensing their desperation. 'Dan Collins said he would bring it over in the morning. He had Moses with him and said it would save me the trouble of lifting it.' Silence hung in the air.

'Mother, it's grand, really grand,' assured Eily, kissing her mother and putting her arms around her neck. She put water on to boil – God knows, Mother deserved a sup of tea.

'Put on a spud each to bake and we'll all have a bit of dry beef too,' said Mother, trying to cheer them up. She suddenly reached deep into the pocket of her apron and produced four rather battered-looking candles. She lit one and placed it on the table and put the others away on the dresser.

The turf fire burned warmly in the grate and the cottage glowed in the soft golden light of the candle. This was home, safe and sound. Spuds baking, it was almost like old times. Peggy sat on Mother's lap, her thin face pressed to Mother's breast.

'Tell us a story, Mother, about when you were little before ...' Peggy stopped. 'Please, Mother.'

Mother kissed her hair and told Michael and Eily to sit in near the fire. She was tired, but it was nice to remember.

'Did I ever tell you about the time of my eighth birthday? Such a time, it was just lovely. My mother, your grandmother, had worked at making me the loveliest dress ever – it was sprigged cotton and had the pattern of pale pink rosebuds against grey on it. It buttoned up the back and had a high collar with a lace ruffle and a lace petticoat to match. The day before, we called to my aunts Nano and Lena in their shop to invite them for tea. I can still see them standing in their white starched aprons, and fruit and pies and tarts spread out on the counter, and the shelf stacked with jams and preserves. Lords and ladies and gentlefolk and big farmers came from far afield to buy their confections and it was said that on market days you would hardly fit into the shop it was that busy. The aunts got very flushed when we walked in, and Mother winked at them.

'On my birthday morning Mother and Father gave me a big package – I can still see it. I tore off the paper and inside there was a doll, a beautiful wooden doll with a proper face and hair, and, would you believe it, she had the same dress as mine and even the same pink ribbon in her hair. Oh, the wonder of it!

'And then, later, a special tea. My Aunt Kitty and my four cousins came to tea. There were scones and fresh-baked bread and plum jam, and then Nano and Lena came and they had a tin with a special cake in it. It was covered in sugar icing and had tiny sweet violets laid on the top. I don't think I've ever seen anything as nice. We all clapped. Aunt Nano had baked the cake and Aunt Lena had decorated it. They were a great pair. Afterwards Father took out the fiddle and we all danced. My three brothers were as nice as pie and didn't fight or shout all evening, and my Aunt Kitty gave us all a dancing lesson.'

Mother stopped. Three soft little faces were turned to her. She swallowed a lump in her throat. Would her little ones ever know such times? Their lives were so hard.

'Come on, children, stir yourselves, the meal is ready.'

They savoured each mouthful, not caring that the potato was so hot it nearly burned their tongues. They cracked the crisp skin. They chewed the dry salted beef, washing it all down with a large mug of milk each. What a feast. They needed no cake after such a feast.

Eily and Michael cleared up and Mother helped Peggy undress for the night. The fire burned low and the candle cast flickering shadows on the wall. How Mother laughed when she heard about Michael, and praised them all on their level-headedness in the face of trouble. Peggy had dozed off. Mother carried her to the bed and tucked her in before settling down again.

'Mother, what about the village?' enquired Eily, wondering why Mother had avoided mentioning it all evening.

'Oh, *a ghile*, what times have fallen on us all. Half the place is dying with the fever and the others have left their houses and taken to the roads, looking for work and food or just to escape the place. The whole O'Brien family is gone.'

'You mean gone on the road, Mother?' interrupted Eily.

'No, *a stór*, into the ground every single one of them, all those five sons and Mary O'Brien, the kindest woman that ever lived. The Connors and Kinsellas have both left. Nell Kinsella had enough put by, and they plan to buy tickets and sail to America. No one knows where the Connors are. Francie O'Hagan has closed up her draper's shop.

She said what call would folk have for material and lace and clothing when they have hardly enough to put a bit of food in their children's mouths.

'Patsy Murphy, in the general store, was packed out – his store room was full of clothes and furniture and knick-knacks. You had to wait in a queue for your turn. There were two women with nothing to trade and not a penny either. Patsy is a good man, he gave them a few scoops of yellow meal each. I had to bargain with him. He could see the fineness of the lacework and could tell Mother was a craftswoman – I put the combs in to seal the deal. All through the village there is hardly a sinner – not a child to be seen outdoors. The strange thing is there seem to be no animals either, the only ones I saw were Patsy's horse and cart and Dan's old Moses. Even the dogs have disappeared.

'Poor Father Doyle is very bad and hasn't stirred at all in weeks – his housekeeper Annie died a few days back. The few men that are left were sitting by the fire in Mercy Farrell's, and not even one was having a sup of porter. I met Corney Egan – that poor man is nothing but a bag of bones. They wouldn't take him for the roadworks, so there is nothing for him now. He told me that the roadworks were about twenty miles from the village and that a lot of the men around about are working there. He thinks that John is one of them. Imagine, your Father may be so near, and working. I should go to him and see if he is all right. He doesn't know about Bridget or how bad things have got.

'There is so much talk. Lord Edward Lyons and all his family have left and gone back to England and closed up the big house – only old Mags and her husband have been left to caretake the place. Jer Simmonds has total control over the farm and land and can do what he likes about the lot of us. Tom Daly is his right-hand man. All the rest of the staff have been let go. Dan told me his daughter Teresa and son Donal have arrived back home as they've nowhere else to go. The world has gone crazy. To think – in a beautiful country like this, people are starving, children hungry. Men and women like ghosts walking the road and all afraid of catching the fever. Has the good Lord forgotten us?'

Eily felt a chill run down her back. She had never heard her gentle Mother talk so much or seem so upset and angry. Eily did not know what to say.

'Then, Father is alive, he might come back to us with money and food and all kinds of things,' blurted out Michael.

'Michael, lovey, the roadworks are far far away. The men are weak and the work is hard. Your father is a strong hardy man, but breaking stones is the very divil. He'll do his best for us all, that I can promise you. You miss him, we all miss him – say a prayer for him when you go to sleep tonight.'

With that Mother got up and went outside. Eily followed her. The sky was black and hundreds of stars twinkled up above.

'Sometimes I wonder does God even know what is happening down here – his world is so vast and big,' whispered Eily.

Mother reached out and put part of her shawl around Eily.

'I know, pet, I wonder too. God acts in such strange ways and there is no sense to why life is so hard. We just have to make the best of what we have and each other and keep going,' she said. She wrapped the shawl tightly around Eily, protecting her from the damp air. Eily had never felt so close to Mother.

CHAPTER 4

On Their Own

 THE NEXT FEW DAYS were busy. Michael went fishing in the river with Pat and his big brother Donal. They were away all day. Michael came home soaked to the skin, his teeth chattering. But, much to everyone's surprise, from under his shirt he produced a large trout. They feasted on it for two days.

After a tip from Dan Collins, Eily and Mother rose very early on two mornings and walked up to the old cow pasture, to discover about a hundred wild mushrooms! With the addition of a spring onion added to the old yellow meal, they made a tasty enough dish. The rest of the mushrooms were despatched to Mary Kate's for drying, as she often used them for her various potions. In exchange she gave them a full can of goat's milk from Nanny, her only remaining goat.

Mother seemed restless and every day stood at the bottom of the lane, watching and waiting for an hour or so. The children pretended not to notice when she turned and walked slowly back to the cottage with tears in her eyes. After five days she told the children she was going to find Father.

'I have to go to the works and find out what has happened. He may be sick or not be able to come for us. We have nothing left to trade or sell – how will we survive without help? It will be like the last time, but it may take a day or two.'

Eily was shocked by the enormity of her Mother leaving them, but accepted her decision.

'Dan and Kitty will keep an eye on ye, but ye can't go down to stay there as Teresa is coughing and I don't want to take any chances. There's enough to eat.' An hour or two later, Mother took her heavy shawl and some food in her pockets and set off. They walked down to the end of the boreen with her. She hugged them each in turn.

'Michael, my little man,' said Mother, ruffling his hair, 'and Eily, the little Mother, and Peggy, my baby – God keep ye safe.'

Eily could see Michael was upset. He kept biting his lip until it nearly bled. Peggy was like a wildcat. She clung to Mother and screamed and fought when Mother tried to leave her. Michael and Eily had to hold her by the waist. The screaming quietened to huge sobs and she lay limp on the ground. They half-carried and half-dragged her back to the cottage. Her eyes and face were swollen with crying. Eily knew exactly how she felt and wished that she was still a small child and could scream and shout and let all her feelings out. But she was twelve and as the eldest had to take Mother's place. For the rest of the day Peggy clung to her like a shadow. They all went to bed early, cuddling up together under the blankets.

'I miss Mother, I want her. I want her now,' cried Peggy.

'Shush, Peggy. Shush, you must rest,' said Eily reassuringly.

'Tell me a story, Eily.'

'I'm not so good on stories, Peggy.'

'One of Mother's stories about when she was young, and the aunts,' pleaded Peggy.

Eily racked her brains. She smiled. 'Did you ever hear tell about the two aunts and why they never married and ended up spinsters?' began Eily.

Peggy relaxed against her.

'Well, the two aunts were still living on the farm – this was before the shop – and they both got to know a fine young farmer called Ted Donnelly – he was a friend of their brothers. He liked them both, even though they were opposites. Aunt Nano was small and plump with brown curly hair, and Aunt Lena was tall and thin with straight black hair. He started to court them. He had a big farm and was an only son. Well, the two aunts were both determined to marry him. Aunt Nano invited him to tea and the table was laden with a feast she had prepared – meat pies and bread and an apple tart and a fruit cake. However, the next week Aunt Lena went on a picnic with him and provided cooked chicken and scones and sweet cake and all kinds of fine things. Week in, week out, he had lunch or tea on the farm and they both made cakes for him, and his mother too called to visit.

'But then a strange thing happened. There wasn't sight nor sound out of him for a few weeks. Then Peadar, their brother, came and told them that Ted was getting married to a girl called Nellie Donovan. She could neither cook nor sew, but was the ideal wife for him. She would be frugal in the kitchen and let his mother continue to run the house as she always had without interference, while she would help with the livestock and the hard work of the farm.

'The two aunts were heartbroken for a few days, but then one day after Sunday lunch they announced that they had spotted an empty shop in Castletaggart town near the market, and with their savings and allowances they were going to rent it and open a speciality shop. Their father opened and closed his mouth and did not know what to say, but his two stubborn daughters would not change their minds.

"Marriage is not for us," they both insisted, and over the years if anyone mentioned men, they always murmured, "Remember Ted Donnelly; he ended up with five fine straps of sons but his home was the dirtiest and shabbiest in the district."'

Eily looked down. Peggy's eyes had shut and Michael was rolled up in a ball in the middle of the blankets.

All the next morning they kept waiting for Mother's return, but she didn't come.

Eily was just in the middle of melting some lard and meal when the clatter of horses' hooves came up the lane. They could see it was the overseer, Jer Simmonds. He worked for the landlord and was in charge of all the tenants. With him was his assistant, Tom Daly. What did they want? The children kept still.

'Open up the door,' shouted Jer, 'else we'll break it in on ye.' Eily got up to open the latch. Anyway, perhaps they had news of Mother.

She stood in the doorway, the other two hiding behind her.

'Where are your Mother and Father?' he shouted.

She was frightened.

'Hold on, now, hold on, don't be fussing her. This is John and Margaret O'Driscoll's place, and you must be the eldest, Ellen is it?' coaxed Tom Daly.

'I'm Eily, begging your pardon,' was all she managed to say.

'Are your parents sick with the fever? Has anyone died in the family?' questioned Jer Simmonds.

'No, they're fine, but our little sister Bridget died a while back. Father is gone on the roadworks. We heard tell that he is on the far side of the village,' she answered.

'Where is Margaret, your mother?' asked Tom Daly.

Eily looked at him. Most people said he was a

fair man and that he often appealed to Jer or the master, Sir Edward, on behalf of a poor tenant. His cheeks were ruddy, and despite his fine clothes and airs he was still only a farmer at heart.

'Mother is gone to look for him. I'm minding the place. She should be back later today.'

Tom accepted her answer. Jer Simmonds started to remount his horse.

'The master and family have left this God-forsaken island and gone back to England. There is no work for anyone now. I am ordered to check all the cottages and send those to the workhouse that have no man or means of keeping themselves. Tell your mother we'll call again tomorrow. If she has disappeared you can't stay here on your own, and will have to make ready for the journey.'

The two men turned their horses, and Eily's face flamed as she knew they were discussing their situation while they walked the horses through the fields.

'What do they mean about the workhouse, Eily?' asked Michael, his face filled with worry.

'Mother will be home soon, so don't be getting yourself in a state,' assured Eily.

The hours dragged by and night fell without any word or sign of Mother. Eily could not sleep a wink with worry and did her best to hide it from the others. During the night it began to rain heavily. The rain battered against the thatch and the water seeped in under the door.

God help Mother, don't let her be out in this, thought Eily.

The next day every hour dragged. None of them had the heart for anything. At midday Tom Daly called to the cottage.

'There's no sign, Eily, is there?' he questioned. She shook her head dumbly. 'You know what it means. Jer will never stand for three children having a cottage to themselves. You probably haven't enough food for more than a few days anyway, then what's to become of you? The workhouse isn't the worst. These are terrible times – I've seen some awful sights. There will be a crowd on the walk. We'll be leaving tomorrow about mid-morning. Be ready, Eily. I'm sorry, but there's no other way,' he finished.

As soon as he left, Eily ran in to the cottage and flung herself on the bed. Tears flooded her face and she could hardly breathe, as wave after wave of misery washed over her. Peggy and Michael stood watching her, round-eyed and terrified to see their big sister lose control. Sensing their fear, she tried to calm herself.

Mother and Father must both be dead – the awful thought pounded in Eily's head. They would never forget about us unless the worst had happened, she thought. She must hide it from the others, they must have hope. She remembered how upset Peggy was when Bridget died and when Mother left. She tried to clear her head to think.

'I'll be all right. Just get me a sup of water, Michael, like a pet,' she asked, as she dried her eyes and wiped her nose.

'What does it mean, Eily?' Michael's young face was pale with worry, his large dark eyes filled with fear.

'I don't know, dotes, I don't know. Maybe something has happened to Mother or Father and they can't get back for a while,' she assured them.

'But Eily, the workhouse! I'd be split from you and Peggy, and we'd all be separated from Mother and Father. Dan Collins told Pat and me the places are full of disease and that you can hear the people screaming when you walk by. I'll not go. I'll take my chance,' said Michael in defiance.

'If Michael's not going, I'll not go,' copied Peggy,

her face solemn as she reached for her brother's hand.

Eily could feel her heart heavy. 'But where will we go then? We can't stay here.'

'What about our friends?' queried Michael. 'The Collinses or Mary Kate?'

'Michael, think, please think,' said Eily. 'The Collinses are good neighbours, but Teresa has the fever and Mrs Collins isn't well either. How could they feed and keep an extra three? And as for Mary Kate – she has a good heart, but her cottage is tiny and she barely has enough to keep herself and Nanny, her goat, and her old dog Tinker.'

They all fell silent.

'What about the relations?' piped up Peggy.

Eily and Michael both turned to her.

'Not grandmother and grandfather in heaven, and we don't know about Auntie Kitty, but the aunts that made the cake?' she carried on. 'The ones in all the stories. They'd have us.'

'You mean the grandaunts, Nano and Lena, in Castletaggart? But that's so far away. How could the three of us make such a journey? I remember the time Grandmother was sick and dying and Mother went back home to see her. It took her days to get there, and she travelled by pony and trap.

We'd have to walk – it would take us weeks, and anyway how would we find our way? And something could have happened to the aunts.' Eily tried to keep the hopelessness out of her voice.

'It's better than the workhouse,' suggested Michael. 'They are family, and Mother and Father could come and get us there. Please, Eily, we've got to stay together.'

Later in the day Eily tried as best she could to tidy the cottage. She washed all the heads, but left the combing and just brushed the hair, and they sat in front of the fire to dry it out. They all fell asleep early in the evening.

Eily woke with a start when the dawn was breaking. She jumped out of bed and ran to the door. Perhaps Mother had arrived back and couldn't get in with them all asleep. Outside all was still – not even a blade of grass stirred. In the far distance she could see a fox running through the fields, a young rabbit hanging limply from its mouth. The birds were beginning to sing. It was another day. She walked down a bit of the boreen, looking back to the cottage. The dirty thatched roof, the two large flat stones outside the door that Mother and Father used as seats on the warm summer evenings. The plot at the side that used to grow vegetables and herbs when times were good. The hedgerow all around and the big hawthorn trees at the back. It was home. How could they ever leave it?

If only Mother were there to tell them what to do. But Mother wasn't coming back. It was just the three of them now. They would survive.

No workhouse for them! They'd find their way to the aunts. In the town of Castletaggart there would be someone who knew them, who belonged to them. Eily took a few deep breaths, filling her lungs with the good fresh air of home. There was work to be done, even though her stomach was groaning with hunger. Mother had called her 'the little Mother'. She would look after Michael and Peggy.

'Up, you lazy lumps,' she scolded, back indoors. 'There's work to be done.'

Peggy rubbed her eyes. She looked tired and pasty. 'Is Mother back yet, Eily?' she asked, still half asleep.

'No, pet, she's not,' hushed Eily, 'but I'm here to take care of you. Would you like to go to the aunts?'

'Yes, oh yes,' pleaded Peggy.

'Outside with the two of ye and then we'll work out a plan,' said Eily.

They all dressed quickly.

'Michael, you must go down to Collinses and tell them what's happened – now, not just that scatter-brain Pat, but his parents. Make sure you tell them that we're going to the two grandaunts, but that Tom Daly thinks he's bringing us to the work-house. The aunts Nano and Lena, just in case Mother and Father come back looking for us. Make sure they understand, but not a word to anyone else,' warned Eily.

Peggy and herself sorted out the few scraps of clothes they had and took the warmest things. They rolled up all the blankets.

At last Michael came back and they could see he had been crying.

'Well, what happened?' asked the girls.

'Teresa passed on yesterday,' he sobbed. 'I couldn't see Pat. He's sick now. He's my best friend in the whole world and I might never see him again. I told Mr Collins, and he said whatever happened he'd make sure Mother heard about us.'

Eily and Peggy prepared a few spuds and a bit of leftover meal. They all sat down. The food tasted like sawdust in their mouths. Would this be their last meal in the cottage? was the big question on all their minds.

Afterwards they cleared up. Carefully they

wrapped the frying pan and two tin cans and a ladle and a blade inside the blankets. They each had a bundle to carry. The remaining food was divided up and hidden in their pockets.

'What if Mother and Father come back and everything is gone – what will they think?' asked Michael.

'They'll know we had to survive. It's better than us all staying, with no food and the disease all around us,' said Eily, trying to make herself believe it.

They sat outside on the stone seat. Suddenly Eily jumped up.

'Bridget, what about Bridget?' she pleaded.

They all ran up to the back field. The grass was covered with wild flowers. The hawthorn tree stood tall, its dark branches heavy with foliage.

A feeling of peace washed over them. They all joined hands and asked Bridget, their little sister, to look after them and keep them safe. They could almost hear her chuckles through the swaying leaves.

'We'll always remember this place,' they swore.

'Come on, you children,' shouted Tom Daly. He was standing at the bottom of the field. 'I can't wait forever for ye.' They gathered up their belongings and Eily closed out the door after them. They walked down the boreen to where a small group of about fourteen people stood.

The children did not speak or look back.

CHAPTER 5

The Road to the Workhouse

THE THREE CHILDREN WALKED for over a mile without uttering a word. They silently looked around at the group. There was Statia Kennedy and her daughter Esther. They were both so weak they could hardly walk. Their eyes were sunken in their heads. And big John Lynch – most people roundabouts knew that although he was a fine big man he only had the mind of a child, and his older sister had always seen after him up to now. Little Kitty O'Hara, walking along on her own, all belonging to her gone. And the O'Connell twins. There were a few old ones, obviously bewildered and upset at having to leave their homes.

Eily fell into step with Kitty O'Hara. She seemed sullen and hostile instead of her usual friendly self.

'Don't say anything, Eily O'Driscoll. I'm glad to be going to the workhouse. At least there'll be a meal and a roof over our heads. They're all gone, every single one. I'm the only one left and I'm going to live.'

Eily did not try to reply. At any other time or in any other circumstances they all might have enjoyed the walk. It was a warm sunny day. The countryside looked green and lush, fine green pasture land all around. The cows, busy chewing, ignored the passersby. Wherever the cows were, a boy or man stood guard to protect them from the poor and starving of the district. At dusk they were locked in and minded for the night.

The cottages and cabins shone white against the hillside. At times a woman standing in her doorway would spot the ragged group walking along. Most just turned around and shut their door. Others threw their aprons over their heads and ran away from such an unlucky sight. Children peeped out and waved. Eily felt ashamed – like an outcast. No one uttered a greeting or a kind word of comfort to the sorry band.

They stopped for a few minutes at a little brook and all had a sip of water or threw it on their faces to refresh themselves. Tom Daly avoided their eyes and seemed preoccupied. Statia Kennedy slipped off her rough boots and was bathing her foot.

Once again they began to walk. Peggy started to whine, but when she saw the fierce glare in Eily's eyes forced herself to stop.

'Don't you dare draw attention to us with your snivelling, Miss, or I'll give you a right belt, do you hear?'

'Yes, Eily, I'm sorry,' murmured Peggy quietly, sensing that she had to behave herself.

They had almost left Duneen, the district they knew so well – another few miles would bring them to the workhouse.

'Oh! Mother of God, my poor old foot!' Statia Kennedy was lying on the ground, her daughter helping her and a few old ones all around her. She dragged off the old leather boots. The dirty black toes were bleeding and sore, the foot puffed and swollen. The old woman was moaning in pain.

Eily winked at Michael. He casually jumped over a low stone wall and walked toward a clump of bushes as if he had to answer a call of nature. In a minute he was out of sight.

The two girls stood still as Tom Daly walked back and knelt down beside the old woman.

'Let me die here along the road, for I'll never

make it to the workhouse,' Statia sobbed.

Tom Daly was trying to soothe and calm her. All eyes were watching him to see what he would do now.

Quick as a flash, Eily jerked Peggy's arm and half-dragged and half-threw her over the stone wall. They bent double and made their way to the bushes. There the three of them wove their way behind the hedgerows and fields. They crossed more stone walls. Gradually they began to make their way uphill, trying to keep hidden.

'Eily, Eily, for heaven's sake come back.'

She could hear Tom Daly calling her name in the distance down below. The three of them kept running. Their hearts hammered in their chests and their breath came in gasps. When they had reached the far side of the hill they slowed down. They had in fact doubled back and were on familiar ground. There was silence all around except for the screech of a bird in the sky. They stopped to rest. From the knees down, their legs were covered in nettle rash. Obviously they had run through the nettles without realising it.

'Michael! Michael!'

It was the O'Connell twins, Seamus and Peadar, identical, with their red curly hair and bright green eyes. They were moving towards them but luckily hadn't spotted them. Quick as lightning the children got down low on their stomachs and managed to drag themselves into a large clump of bracken and gorse. The fields and hillsides were covered with gorse, its vivid yellow flowers making bright smudges on the landscape. It was thorny and spiky, and tore their hands and cut their faces. Even through their clothes it scratched their skin. They lay still, not daring even to breathe. Now they understood the fear of a petrified rabbit or hare cornered in the bushes.

Peadar stood a few feet away from them. He had a thin stick in his hand. He brought it down sharply on the gorse, making the whole clump move. Eily kept her eyes tightly shut.

'Shamey, Shamey, there's no sight of them. How long does Tom want us to search for them before we catch him up on the road?' They had moved away a bit by now and were complaining to each other. The voices seemed more distant, but Michael insisted that they stay put just in case it was a trap. Eily was so crouched that her toes and feet had gone numb. A large prickle was pressing against her back. She had to force herself to lie still.

Peadar's voice suddenly got louder and a third

person had joined them. Had Tom Daly come himself to search for them? No, it wasn't a man's voice. They knew the voice. It was Mary Kate. Another twenty minutes or so passed and there wasn't a sound. Was it safe to come out?

'Nanny, Nanny. Will you show yourself, you bothersome creature? I'm worn out with you,' cajoled Mary Kate. The old woman was looking for her goat. That would explain her being up the back fields.

'Oh Nanny, you have my poor old heart broken,' wailed Mary Kate.

Eily could see her through the bushes and could hardly believe her eyes – Mary Kate was winking, or was there something wrong with her eye? No, she was definitely winking. The old lady was standing in front of them.

'Nanny, Nanny,' she shouted out loud, then in a low voice whispered, 'You're all right now, you spalpeens, I've sent them on a wild goose chase. Come out of there quick and we'll go back to my place.'

They could hardly believe their ears or eyes. They were stiff and sore, but still had to keep low until they came to Mary Kate's cottage. She pushed them inside and then closed the door.

They blinked in the gloom, trying to get used to the darkness after the bright sunshine outside. Once inside, Mary Kate hugged each of them in turn. They told her the whole story and how they had managed to escape from being sent to the workhouse. She tut-tutted and said how brave they were. While they talked she got water and a cloth and busied herself bathing and cleaning their scratches and nettle stings. Then with two grimy fingers she smeared a greasy ointment on the affected parts. It smelled foul, like something rotten, but within about two minutes all the pain and stinging had eased. The cottage was filthy, as usual, and Eily was tempted to take the broom and give it a good sweep out in order to repay the old lady's kindness in sheltering them. With the four of them inside there was scarcely room to move. The children squatted on the floor among the ashes and dirt. Mary Kate began to poke at the fire and put a large pot on to cook.

'Children, you know you are welcome here with me,' said Mary Kate.

Eily knew she meant it, but it would be impossible to stay there as the place was far too small and Mary Kate was used to having it to herself. Also there would be the risk that Tom Daly would find out they were there and maybe evict the old lady.

'We'll stay the night, Mary Kate,' said Eily, trying not to sound ungrateful, 'but at first light tomorrow we must set off on our journey to Castletaggart to find our aunts. We don't know what has happened Mother and Father, but they'll come after us if they can.'

Peggy had begun to relax and found she was no longer afraid of the old lady, and she sat at Mary Kate's feet, petting Tinker. A delightful smell came from the pot and filled the air. The children's stomachs groaned with hunger. Mary Kate got four plates from under a pile of rubbish. She wiped them with her sleeve and then ladled out the piping hot mixture. Eily and Michael couldn't work out exactly what it was, but it tasted grand and maybe it was better not to ask what was in it, as God only knows what the old woman had managed to collect for her cooking pot.

Then Mary Kate tucked Peggy up in her settle bed. Afterwards she sat down in her old chair and chatted to Michael and Eily. She got two or three jars down and took off the lids.

'This one is for the fever. You mix it with water and drink it about four times a day,' began Mary

Kate. 'This one is for stomach ache and cramps. You take a pinch of the leaves and herbs and chew them – never mind the taste. And this is the one I used tonight. It is for cuts and wounds, bites and stings. First of all, you must clean the wound well and then put on the ointment.'

She replaced the lids and gave them to Eily. 'You have a long journey ahead, let nature be your friend and help. Keep away from other people on the roads, for they will carry the sickness. Keep close to the river as it will help you to find your way. Gather what you may from the countryside, but don't eat strange berries or mushrooms and don't eat any dead animal you find. Only fresh meat is good. God keep ye safe, ye poor creatures. I'll be thinking of ye and will keep an eye out for your mother.'

Having said her piece, the old lady got up and pulled off the top two layers of her clothes and got into bed beside the sleeping Peggy. Eily and Michael were so exhausted and tired they lay down to sleep on the ground.

The dawn was just breaking when they got ready to take their leave of Mary Kate. A drink of goat's milk and some stale soda bread was their breakfast. Two large tears ran down the old lady's cheeks, creating a pale streak in the brown face. They all knew it was unlikely they would ever meet again.

'God spare ye,' prayed Mary Kate, and waved as they walked through the long dew-soaked grass and headed down towards the flash of blue in the distance through the trees. For there lay the river.

CHAPTER 6

Follow the River

IT WAS STILL COOL in the early morning as they walked through the damp grass. Later on, the day promised to be a scorcher. They could almost pretend they were off on an adventure for a few hours. One or two startled rats ran across their path. They made their way carefully through a field of oats. Tall thin bright red poppies grew there and waved at them. Peggy could not resist the temptation and began to pull them, but within a few minutes they hung limply from her hands and the soft red petals clung damply together. It was best to leave them swaying gently in the slight breeze.

It took them about an hour to reach the river.

They sat on the rocks and dangled their feet in the cold clear water that rushed over the stones and sand. They followed its course for the next two hours, but the ground was getting heavier and soggier and their feet kept getting stuck in the oozing mud. The field all around them was damp and they kept sinking in the clinging soil. Across the river the grass seemed drier and they could see no signs of the rough holes filled with stagnant water that they kept trying to avoid.

'We must cross the river,' urged Michael. 'Otherwise we might get stuck and have to take to high ground.' His voice was serious and he kept his eyes peeled until at last he considered he'd found an easy spot.

The river narrowed and large lichen-covered rocks made a pathway in the middle of the rushing water.

'I'll go across first, girls, to show you the way,' Michael teased, 'and then I'll come back for Peggy.' He waded out to the first rock. It was uneven, and wobbled dangerously. He hopped to the next, which was long and narrow, and then two little ones, then a high step up on to a jagged piece of granite. From there it was easy to jump neatly from one to the other until you reached the sand and gravel on the other side. Michael bowed with bravado at them. 'Now, isn't that easy? Peggy, I'll come back for you.'

Peggy waded out a bit and then followed Michael's directions. When the big rock wobbled she was sure she would fall in, but Michael stretched out his arm to steady her. All was going well until they reached the jagged rock. Michael had to go ahead of her and help pull her on to it. As he leaned towards her he suddenly realised that he had gashed his shin and that the blood was dripping into the crystal clear water. Eily had come after them and was only two stones behind. A few seconds later they were safe at the water's edge.

'Michael, you've cut yourself,' said Eily. 'Will I get Mary Kate's stuff?'

He shrugged. 'I'll just wash it, it's only a nick. Don't be fussing – you're nearly as bad as Mother.'

They began to walk again. Under their breath they hummed a tune of Father's. Peggy kept stopping to pick up stones and flowers and old bird feathers, but when no-one would help her carry them she had no choice but to drop them along the way. They walked for a few hours. The sun was high and directly over their heads. The sweat ran down their foreheads and the back of their necks.

'I want to stop, I'll not go another foot,' insisted Peggy. Her cheeks were hot and flushed and she looked dead tired.

They all flopped down to rest. Mary Kate had given them a canful of Nanny's milk. They all had a few sups of it. With this heat, in another few hours it would be undrinkable. There was some cold meal mix. That was enough, they would save the rest for later. They rinsed out the can in the river and filled it with water, then they lay back in the sunshine like a crowd of kittens. They were so tired they did not even have the energy to talk. Eily did not know how it happened, but they must all have dozed off, for when she woke up the sun was lower in the sky and the heavy heat was gone from it. She thumped the others to wake-up and get on their way as they should aim to walk another few miles before dusk.

Later they found a safe dry place still within sight of the river, and spread the blankets on the soft bracken. A bit more to eat, then they cuddled up close and watched the night sky creep in. They were fast asleep before the stars appeared.

The next three days continued in much the same

way. Eily was only too conscious that the food bag was getting lighter and lighter. Michael's 'little nick' had not healed up. Yellow pus was beginning to appear under the scab and light pink streaks ran from it up towards his knee. They had all slowed down, but Eily suspected that Michael might even be in pain. The night before, despite all his giving out, she had put a dollop of Mary Kate's ointment on the skin, hoping they hadn't left it too late.

On that fourth day the air was hot and heavy, but there was no sign of the sun. It was exhausting to walk in such weather as you felt there was not enough air to fill your lungs.

Through the rushes and weeds that covered the river bank, they could at times glimpse people on the distant road. As the ground near the river was stonier, Eily felt it might be easier for Michael to walk on the well-worn path. They passed a few other people on the path, but avoided them, remembering Mary Kate's warning. Then a man came by on horseback, pulling a slide. He had a piece of cloth tied around his face, his eyes stared straight ahead. On the slide were piled four or five skeleton-like bodies, their bare skin and bones showing through the rags. The children moved away, turning their backs. Eily clamped the palms of her hands over Peggy's eyes, trying to protect her from such a sight.

Dejectedly they kept on going, and after a few miles they came upon a carriage. A horde of people surrounded it, silent and threatening. The driver was trying to calm the terrified horse as two very shaken passengers took in the frenzy around them. They were afraid for their lives. The man stood up and scattered coins on the ground, hoping to disperse the crowd and clear a path. The woman had lost her bonnet and was pale with shock at the desperate appearance of the men, women and children all around.

Frightened by these things, the children slipped off the road and on to a trail which ran in the same direction as the river. Eily could not stop herself longing for Father and Mother and wondering what might have happened to them.

By next morning, Michael's leg had swollen and he could not bend his knee. They would not be able to get very far with such a setback. He managed to hobble for about a mile. Then they had such luck they could hardly believe it. They had just crossed a stile when at the far end of the field, under a clump of huge chestnut trees, they noticed a little spiral of smoke. Peggy ran on ahead.

'It's a fire,' she called. 'Come on quick and see.'

She was right. They could hardly believe it – the dying embers of a fire! Eily frantically scrambled around under the trees looking for some dry twigs. She found a few and carefully put them on the embers, then knelt down and began to blow softly. A slight flicker of flame began to stir. Peggy was jumping up and down with excitement. Suddenly a finger of flame touched the dryness of the twigs and set them alight. They had a fire. Michael lowered himself down gently to the ground and positioned himself against the broad trunk of one of the trees, his legs stretched out in front of him. The girls put down their things and then set out to search for anything that would fuel the fire. They kept going backwards and forwards with the twigs and sticks, until they felt they had enough to keep it going.

Obviously some other people had passed this way not so long before. There were other signs of their presence too. Eily searched the long grass until she found the thick blackened branch that they must have used for the fire. She hung the pot from it and poured in some water and a piece of lard, then two handfuls of the yellow meal. She also set three wizened-looking spuds to bake in the embers. Tonight they would eat well, as they were all famished and getting weaker and would need strength to search for food.

Although the weather was warm, it was lovely to feel the heat of the fire and to smell something cooking. Michael looked dead tired. For once he had to rest easy and let the girls do all the work. The meal began to burn and Eily had to scrape it out of the pot, but still it was good to have something warm inside your stomach. She put the pot on again to boil some water.

'What's that for?' queried Michael. 'Is there more to eat?' he asked hopefully.

'You strap,' joked Eily, 'and I've no big wooden spoon here. Will you whisht. It's for yourself, for the leg, and if you're good there'll be a baked spud after.'

It didn't take long for the water to boil.

'What are you going to do, Eily?' Michael asked, his voice fearful.

'Something I've seen Mother do a few times,' she replied. 'Do you remember when Father got that splinter in his hand, and when Peggy got that bad gash on her knee? Michael, the wound is full of poison. We've got to get rid of it and clean it out.'

She lifted the pot off the fire and set it on a stone.

She got the blade and held it in the water for about two minutes and then quickly laid it against the vicious cut on his leg for a few seconds. Michael screamed with the pain. Then she dropped the blade and tore a strip of cloth from her spare shift. She dipped it in the water, then tied it over the wound and around the leg.

'It's too hot. Take it off, take it off, Eily,' begged Michael.

'No, it's got to stay,' she replied sternly as she began to tear up another strip of cloth and soak it in the water, hoping her little brother wouldn't notice the tears in her eyes.

She changed the dressing three times, and the third time the cloth was stained yellow and green where the pus was draining away. She poured the still fairly hot water over the leg, washing the wound out and finally she tied a dry strip of cloth over it.

The next morning Eily breathed a sigh of relief when she saw Michael. The swelling had gone down and the vivid red streaks that ran up his leg had now faded to a dusty pink. She forbade him to stand on the leg, and made him rest it as she boiled some more water and replaced the strips of cloth.

The most urgent thing now was to get more

water and fuel, and if possible something to eat. Eily made her way down towards a stream she had noticed a while back, to refill the cans. She did not trust Peggy, first of all not to fall into the water and then not to spill it all running back. Peggy was dispatched to search for more firewood, and if she saw anything edible to remember where. However, she had to stay within shouting distance of Michael.

On the way back, Eily could not believe her luck when she spotted a clump of tiny wild strawberries, their little red hearts peeping through a mass of nettles and weeds. She would come back for them and also for a few new nettles to add to a bit of soup. Peggy was back before her and ran wild with excitement towards her.

'Eily, Eily, just wait 'till you see what I've got. Come on quickly,' urged Peggy.

Eily placed the water cans in a steady spot, waiting to see what all the fuss was about. Peggy ran behind the tree and emerged with a large rabbit hanging from her hands. Glassy-eyed, it stared at Eily and Michael. It looked like it had been dead for a day or more.

'Where did you get it, pet?' asked Eily gently. 'You didn't catch it yourself?'

'No, Eily, I found it, just lying near a bunch of lovely blue flowers. Isn't. it grand?' Peggy said proudly.

Eily didn't know what to say. God knows they could do with a bit of meat, but she couldn't help but remember Mary Kate's warning about eating only fresh meat and not touching anything they found already dead.

'Peggy, pet, don't you remember what old Mary Kate told us?'

Peggy's face crumpled in disappointment. However, she accepted the sense of Eily's words and ran back into a clump of trees and flung the rabbit away. Eily consoled her by saying that maybe there were a few rabbits around where she had found that one and they might catch one yet. Also, she told her to fetch the pot and she would show her where some baby wild strawberries grew.

The day was spent gathering anything that was vaguely edible and more fuel. Michael wanted to try to walk, but Eily insisted he give the leg another day's rest. They sucked the wild strawberries until their mouths were stained red. Eily also found an untended plot of land with a few stragglers of young carrots and turnips. She filled her pockets, delighted with herself and the thought of the nourishing soup she could now make with just the addition of a sliced spud.

That afternoon the sun was so warm that Peggy and Eily ran off to the river to cool down and waded in as far as their waists, splashing each other and washing the grime off their bare arms and their necks and faces. Then they lay on the river bank in their shifts until the sun had dried them off. That night there was a large helping of soup for everyone and the last of the yellow meal pan-cooked.

The following day, Michael was up before them and standing in front of them, proudly showing that his leg was healed. His walking was a bit stiff, but he was anxious to explore his surroundings. They knew they should move on, but were loath to leave the comforts of the fire. They built it up a bit before showing Michael around.

Peggy brought them to where she had found the rabbit. They huddled down in the bracken and after a very long wait were rewarded with the sight of a family of young rabbits nibbling and playing a few feet away. The children kept perfectly still. Michael had a large stone gripped between his fingers. He had spotted a little one that had strayed too far from the rest, busy nibbling at some juicy grass. Within an instant he had taken aim. At first it seemed that the rabbit was just stunned. All the others had scampered off and disappeared. Then Michael realised how accurate he had been as the rabbit took its last breath. He ran over and lifted it up. It was very small. There wouldn't be much eating in it, but at least it was meat.

Peggy came over to Michael and belted him on the chest. She was clearly upset at seeing the young animal die. Eily made sure to decoy her away when Michael was skinning and cleaning it. However, once Eily had boiled the rabbit with a few carrots and a bit of wild onion, there were no objections from Peggy to such filling fare. That night their stomachs groaned from trying to digest such good nourishing food.

It was still dark when they felt the first specks of rain touch their faces. At about seven o'clock that morning the rain came, heavy and steady. Their fire had gone out, the rain-water washing through the ashes and running in grey rivulets through the grass. They gathered up their belongings. The two girls pulled their shawls up over their heads. There was no point in staying any longer. They had to be on their way again.

CHAPTER 7

The Soup Kitchen

FOR THE NEXT TWO DAYS it rained on and off. All their clothes were damp. Their bones ached. At night they lay on the wet ground trying to find some shelter as they wrapped up in their damp blankets. They had made their way to the road again, as the grass was too wet for walking.

A few times other people passed them by. Most just nodded. They looked miserable – ragged and undernourished and dirty. The children were unaware that they themselves looked just as bad. As luck had it, a tall thin boy of about fifteen fell into step beside them.

'Joseph T. Lucy,' he announced, introducing

himself with a bow. His clothes were filthy and Eily couldn't help but wrinkle her nose as he also smelled of sweat and grime. Despite these failings, he was a good companion, and after about a half an hour Eily relaxed enough to loosen her hold on the near-empty food bag.

Joseph informed them that they were only about an hour from the small village of Kineen. He had heard that some strange religious folk had set up a soup kitchen for the poor of the area there.

'C'mon,' he urged them, 'we might all get a dacent meal and a bit of a rest.'

Joseph was right, it would be good to have a meal, and perhaps they might meet someone they knew and who might have word of Mother and Father. Kineen it was, then.

Eily could not believe the crowds when they reached the village. Hundreds of ragged starving people thronged the small main street. They queued, desperate for food. Some were so weak they could not stand, so they sat on the ground, dejected but determined to keep their place. The children fell into line at the very back. Eily's eyes roved over the crowd, searching to see if she could pick out any familiar face.

The faces – the faces – she would never forget

them. They all had the same look. The cheeks were sunken, the eyes wide and staring with deep circles underneath, the lips narrow and tight, and in some the skin had a yellow tinge. Hunger and sickness had changed these people. Now they were like ghosts. Old women clawed and tried to push their way to get further up the line. Mothers stood staring ahead as scrawny toddlers pulled and whined against their filthy skirts. This must be hell, thought Eily, for once really terrified.

Suddenly in the distance three women with aprons and caps emerged from the doors of a ramshackle shed, lifting a large heavy cauldron. Immediately the crowd surged forward. Eily just managed to grab hold of Peggy, whose feet were actually lifted off the ground in the panic. Peggy fastened her arms around Eily's waist and rested her head against her chest. She was exhausted and scared.

The women had begun to ladle out the soup. There were tin mugs for those who did not have anything of their own. Twice the pot was refilled before the children actually moved forward.

Now Eily had a clearer view. She could make out figures inside the shed busily chopping carrots and turnips and onions and throwing them into large wooden vats, along with scoops of barley and buckets of water. A man then came along with a bucket of roughly chopped pieces of meat and offal and threw them in too.

The afternoon passed and they still had not reached the top. All the children were worried about was that the soup would run out before they had their turn. Finally they got there. An exhausted woman begged one of the servers for two extra mugs for her two children, who were about half a mile back along the road. They were too weak to walk any further. She was refused, but when she took a long gulp of the hot soup from her own mug, the server quickly replaced it with a bit of a top-up. The woman carefully made her way back through the crowds carrying the precious liquid. Eily and Michael and Peggy and Joseph all took a big swallow of the soup too when their turn came, but no top-up was offered. Then they found a free bit of space to sit and enjoy the meal. The soup was greasy and globs of fat floated on its surface, but it would keep them going.

That night they slept in Kineen, as it was rumoured that the soup kitchen would re-open at midday again the next day. During the night an old man shook them and told them to be on their way, as the heathens would try to convert them in the morning and if they took another mug of soup they may as well take the Queen's shilling. The children were puzzled, but simply ignored him.

The following morning they positioned themselves mid-way in the starving group. Gradually they became aware of a kindly-looking gentleman and two women moving among the ragged crowd. At times the younger woman would emerge from the crowd with a young boy or girl in tow, or a toddler in her arms, and make her way to a large house at the end of the village. She would knock at a green door, then disappear inside and re-emerge on her own a few minutes later.

Eily wondered what they were doing. Were they taking the children to some kind of orphanage or workhouse? They were getting nearer and nearer. The older woman had begun to chat to Peggy. She was asking her was she on her own. Peggy turned and pointed out Eily and Michael, then came the next question: 'But where are your parents?'

Eily reached out and pulled at Peggy who was staring blankly at the lady, wondering what she was meant to say. Frantically Eily's eyes scanned the crowd. In the far distance she spotted a red-haired woman sitting on a doorstep, her husband standing beside her.

'There they are, Miss,' replied Eily, quickly pointing out the pair. The old lady looked doubtful. Quickly Eily waved at the red-haired woman. Their eyes met and the woman nodded back at Eily, wondering in her own mind who that lassie with the long fair hair was. The old lady, satisfied, moved on.

Once they had received their portion of the thick mutton stew, they made their way back to the edge of Kineen. The three children felt they wanted to get back on their way, but Joseph pleaded with them to stay, reluctant to lose his new-found friends. They explained to him about the aunts and how they hoped Mother and Father would turn up there. He wanted to stay in Kineen for another few days and then make his way to one of the harbour ports and try to get passage on one of the ships sailing for Liverpool.

It was with heavy hearts that they took leave of one another. Michael had to swallow a lump in his throat as he said yet another goodbye.

CHAPTER 8

Beside the Lake

THE CHILDREN KEPT WALKING ON. Peggy had two huge blisters on her foot. Every few hours Eily smeared the foot with Mary Kate's ointment. For the most part, the skin on the soles of their feet was like blackened leather. Eily's hands were hard and calloused, the skin scarred with the constant weight of all she had to carry. She had developed a touch of 'the flux', and suspected the slightly rancid mutton stew from Kineen. She chewed the herbal remedy of Mary Kate's, hoping it would ease her nausea and the cramps in her stomach.

They had stopped for a rest when they became aware of a smell – more like a stench. Even worse than the time the potatoes had rotted.

'Eily, what could it be?' questioned Michael. 'Do you think everything around us is going to rot and die?'

Peggy and Eily made for a clump of bushes to relieve themselves. Suddenly the stench, with an even fouler undertone, washed over them. Eily saw it and turned, hoping that Peggy hadn't noticed, but Peggy's face was white with fear.

It was a man – well, what was left of him. The skin was rotted and all different colours. He was thin, so thin that his bones already showed. Eily could feel pinpricks of sweat across her brow and her stomach turning. Peggy had screwed up her eyes and was pulling at her dress. Almost in unison they got sick in the bushes. Once their stomachs were empty and the heaving had stopped, they galloped back to Michael. One look at their faces and he knew something terrible had happened.

'What is it, girls? What is it?' he kept on.

In between tears and sobbing, they managed to tell him.

'That poor soul,' cried Eily. 'To die all alone in the middle of nowhere, starved and with no family or friends.'

'We must say a prayer for him,' said Michael in a low voice. He broke two twigs and fashioned them into a cross, tying them with some long pieces of grass.

They all walked back towards the bushes.

'I don't want to get sick again,' wailed Peggy, keeping a few steps back behind the others. They stopped short a few yards away from the body. Michael pushed the simple cross into the ground.

'What will we say?' asked Michael.

'An "Our Father",' replied Eily. When it was said, Eily asked God to remember this poor lost man.

As quickly as they could they gathered up their stuff, wanting to get away from that dreadful place, so much so that they did not stop walking until they noticed a towering green forest that stretched for miles. It reminded them of the forest at home near Duneen, and they suddenly realised that it was almost two weeks since they had left home. Seeking comfort, the children slipped off the road and into an almost familiar world. The huge trees reached right up to touch the sky, sounds were muffled and they seemed to be walking on a dull carpet of pine needles and moss. Very little sunlight filtered through, but there in the calm and peace, with only the odd coo of a wood-pigeon, the world seemed a better place.

They kept a good eye on the road in the distance, moving parallel to it. Secure in the forest, they relaxed. The odd small startled animal ran across their path and in the far distance the muffled sound of a fast-running mountain stream could be heard. Time had stopped still in this place. They remembered past times playing hide-and-seek in the woods near home – now they did not have the energy even to run.

After about two hours' walking they all sat down. Peggy and Michael were exhausted. Peggy began to cry, her breath coming in racking sobs. She could not stop. Eily pulled her on to her lap. She could feel how light Peggy was – no sign of the plump young arms and legs. Her skin seemed barely to cover her bones and her ribcage stuck out. Eily laid her head against her little sister's head, and the tears slid soundlessly down her face. A total sense of hopelessness washed over her. Oh how she longed for Mother to come and take care of them all, or Father to tell them what to do.

Michael looked at them. He could feel Eily's sorrow and grief.

'We're going to die like the rest of them, aren't we?' he whispered. He was scared. He had always had so many plans for when he was older. He knelt down beside Eily and they hugged each other. They cried, each voicing their own fears.

'I wanted to play on a hurling team like the big

fellows, and some day learn to ride a horse and maybe even have a place of my own,' said Michael.

'I wanted to have a fine wool dress with a lace collar and combs in my hair. Maybe then when I was older I would fall in love and get married like Mother and have babies of my own,' sobbed Eily.

They looked at Peggy. She had calmed down a bit. 'Just a doll of my own and maybe to go to school and best of all to be like Eily,' she said in a shaky little voice.

Eily held her close, overwhelmed with the love she felt for her brother and sister. She felt her heart would burst with the sadness of it all.

Suddenly Peggy laughed. 'Look at Michael. His face is all blotchy and his eyes are so red.'

Then Michael looked at the girls. Their hair was wild, and they both had runny noses and raw-looking eyes. He half-hiccupped and laughed. Eily couldn't help smiling at the silliness of it all, and within a few seconds they were laughing out loud and blowing their noses.

'What eejits we are,' joked Eily. 'We're still alive. We're tired and hungry and on our own, but we have each other and we can still walk and forage. We'll get to Nano and Lena's even if it takes us a month.'

The bout of crying had released a lot of the tensions and they all felt in some way refreshed and renewed in their purpose.

The forest trail began to climb slightly and they planned to follow it until dusk and spend the night there, knowing that the next morning they would have to get back down to the road.

.

When they did, the road seemed less crowded. Two funerals passed them, and two middle-aged women fell into step with Eily. One carried a wasted-looking baby wrapped inside her shawl. They felt it was their duty to inform Eily of all the latest gossip roundabouts.

'Lovey, did you hear tell of the little village of Dunbarra? The poor old priest went calling on four of the cottages and found all in them dead of the famine fever and huge rats swarming the place. They had to open a burial pit a mile outside the village to throw all the bodies of those that died into it.' The women continued, with each story worse than the one before. Eily felt faint and had to sit down on a hillock of grass. Michael and Peggy came over to see what was wrong. The women, terrified of the fever, quickened their pace and were soon gone. Eily refused to tell the others what had upset her so.

They looked across the fields and in the distance they could see a group of people working. Two men further up the road had crossed the stone wall and were making for that field too. The children decided to follow. As they came nearer to the field, they could clearly see the ragged group kneeling on the ground lifting young turnips. They hurried over. An old man assured them that the farmer, an old bachelor, had died that very morning of the fever and that there was no harm in the poor trying to save themselves. The children split up and began to sink their hands into the damp mud and lift out the small pale turnips and place them in their pockets. Then Eily put them one after another in the food bag. Some poor creatures were eating them as soon as they lifted them, barely knocking the earth off. Eily tried to avert her eyes. Within about half an hour the field had been picked clean, as if it was harvest time. The group then disbanded and all went their separate ways.

At least the food bag was now fairly full, even if it was with food usually reserved for animals. The children kept going overland, climbing over the stone walls. The fields were carpeted with wild flowers and clover, the hum of honey bees droned in the still air. The sun blazed down, drying out the damp earth. They walked for about another two miles and suddenly became aware of the sparkle of the sun reflecting on water. It was a lake, and it stretched as far as the eye could see. High, thin water reeds formed a circle around it and at times there were clear patches of sand and stony gravel over which the clear water lapped.

The children could hardly wait – they dropped all they were carrying and ran into the water. It was bliss. The coolness washed over them. They splashed each other and ducked their heads down under the water, filling their mouths with it and squirting it at each other. Then they got out and lay on the grass, stretching out to bake in the sun, and after about fifteen minutes they charged back into the water to cool down again. On the centre of the lake wild birds dived in and out and bobbed on the calm surface of the water.

Michael looked at the birds fishing. If only he had something to fish with, but he had no line or anything, not even a net. He watched the shallows of the lake and the odd time could make out a fish darting in and out among the water weeds near the rushes, or basking near the lily leaves. But how to catch one? That was the question.

He explained what he wanted to Eily. Suddenly she jumped up and emptied out the filthy sacking that was the food bag.

'This will do, Michael. Go on, have a try!'

Michael looked very doubtful, but he searched around a bit and found a willow tree. Using the blade, he cut a thin branch off it and pulled off the leaves. It was light but strong. He poked it through a small hole near the top of the bag. Then, wading into the water, he lowered the bag so that it filled with water and opened out. He kept it on its side.

Michael did not move. Two or three curious little fish swam past, and at last one went in to investigate. Quickly Michael lifted up the stick and bag, but he saw the fish dart away. He had to wait for the water to settle before beginning the whole procedure all over again. He stood still for about another hour before he was successful. Swiftly he lifted the bag out of the water. The fish struggled and tried to jump back in, but Michael flung the bag to the safety of the shore. The silver fish flipped and flapped and finally was still, giving up the struggle. Straight away Michael started to fish again and twenty minutes later two little sprats had joined the fish on the shore.

Now they had something to eat, but none of them was prepared to eat the fish raw.

'We need a fire,' said Peggy, sure that the others knew what to do. Michael and Eily looked at each other, but they didn't know.

'I remember Pat told me that his father could start a fire by rubbing flint stones together,' suggested Michael.

'Do you think you know what to do?' asked Eily.

Michael scrabbled around till he found two likely-looking stones. The girls gathered up a heap of dry sticks and twigs, then Michael began to rub and then hit the stones off each other. After ten minutes his hands ached and he passed the stones to Eily. It was infuriating. They could see sparks coming off the stones, but just couldn't get them to set the dry timber alight. Eily was just about to throw the stones on the ground with vexation, when she felt a spark burn her finger and realised that it had caught the sticks and was beginning to smoulder. Cautiously she blew and tried to encourage the flame to catch. Suddenly, as if in answer to a prayer, the fire began to burn.

'I knew you could do it,' Peggy declared.

Michael got the blade, cut off the fish heads and split the fish down the middle. Then he washed them in the lake to clean them out.

Within half an hour the fire was burning stead-
ily, and Peggy found a large flat stone which Michael placed at the edge of the fire. The flames
licked around it. The fish lay on the stone, baking
among the embers. Eily hung the pot over the fire
with a little water in it and about six of the small
turnips cut up in chunks. A delicious smell filled
the air and the children said a silent prayer, hoping
that no one was around to discover their meal.
They thought they had never tasted anything like
it. The fish had a slightly burnt flavour and the
turnip was soft and sweet – a meal for a king,
washed down with a can of ice-cold water. That
night they slept, warm and well fed. It was tempting to stay in such an idyllic location and spend a
few days there, but Eily felt it was better to get
moving once more.

CHAPTER 9

The Dogs

THE FOLLOWING DAY the sun baked down again. The ground was dry and hard and Michael poured a can of water on the embers to make sure the fire was out. Eily fixed up the food bag, wrapping the leftover fish in a large leaf. It was a grand day for travelling. They crossed through a field of rye, pulling as many ears as they could, then they moved back up alongside the winding country boreen.

After a while the children became aware of the distant barking of dogs. The sound got closer. From the corner of her eye, Eily spotted the dogs following behind. There were six of them, a crazed-looking lot. Their leader was a large black collie, and there were two other collies and three mongrels. Their hair was matted and filthy and they panted heavily, their mouths hanging open. Their bodies were bony and scrawny, and two of them had the mange. But it was their eyes that frightened Eily. They were mad and staring.

'Don't make any sudden moves,' whispered Eily, 'just walk slow and steady. Don't try to run.'

The three of them were totally petrified. The dogs drew nearer and two of the collies began to circle in and out between their legs. The children froze to the spot, barely daring to breathe. Peggy had closed her eyes tightly. The collie's nose and mouth were close to her upper leg. She began to tremble from head to toe. The dog had bared its teeth and a low growl came from deep within its throat. Two of the mongrels bared their jaws too and joined in the growling.

This was too much for little Peggy to bear. She snapped out of her trance and tried to run, but in a flash the collie had pulled itself up on its forelegs. She pushed it off, but it sank its jaws into her arm and started to drag the limb back and forth as if trying to pull the bone from its socket. Peggy was screaming and howling with pain.

Eily felt paralysed watching what was happening. She could not even get a sound to come from her mouth. The other dogs, emboldened, had moved in. Eily suddenly snapped out of it as Michael flung stones at the dogs. She started to shout at them and pelted a young collie and a vicious-looking mongrel that had only one ear. They barked with the pain. Michael was frantically searching around in the ditch. Eily tried to pull the crazed collie that was holding Peggy by the scruff of the neck, but he would not let go his grip. Peggy was half-kneeling at this stage under the weight and exhaustion. In another few seconds he would have her down on the ground. A small terrier nipped at Eily's heels until they bled.

Suddenly, Eily could hardly believe what she saw. Michael came charging with a short thick branch of a tree. He swung it at the collie, who didn't even notice or care, he was in such a frenzy. Michael began to belt it on the head. Peggy's eyes had closed and her knees were bent under her. Michael kept on hitting and hitting the dog. Finally it yelped with pain, releasing the arm a bit. Michael made a final smash and the animal collapsed dead in the dust.

Eily ran to Peggy. The little girl's face was ashen.

She was too shaken even to cry.

'Oh God, it's all right, pet, he's dead – the rest are gone – you're all right, Peggy, the bad dogs are gone.' Eily didn't know whether she was trying to reassure herself or Peggy.

Michael stood at the side of the road. He was bent over, getting sick after the shock.

Eily got the water can. First of all she held it to Peggy's lips, forcing her to drink some to revive her. Then she poured it over the middle part of her arm, between the wrist and elbow, washing away the blood and saliva. Deep puncture marks made by the teeth covered the arm, and part of the skin had been torn and was bleeding heavily. Luckily, Eily had kept the cloths she had torn for Michael's leg and had washed and boiled them and dried them out. She got some of Mary Kate's ointment, rubbed it in gently and then bandaged up the arm. Peggy's breathing was becoming more regular and a bit of colour was coming back to her face. Eily also bathed the nips on her own heels and put a dab of ointment on them.

Michael sat on the stone wall, his head in his hands. His black curly hair clung damply to his forehead. Eily went over to him and hugged him.

'I don't like killing things, Eily,' he murmured.

'I know, Michael, but you saved Peggy, and anyway that poor demented creature is better off dead,' she said.

'I suppose so,' was his reluctant reply.

Peggy was very scared and shaken, but was ready after about an hour's rest to go on further. If they followed this road they would be in the town of Ballycarbery by morning.

CHAPTER 10

At the Harbour

'MICHAEL, LOOK, DO YOU SEE IT?' Peggy was standing on a fence, pointing towards the sea.

Through gaps in the hedgerows they were able to catch glimpses of bright blueness, speckled with white, and there was a tang in the air. The sun blazed in a vivid blue sky. No cloud or breeze had dimmed its strength for days.

The children felt hot and sticky by the time they reached Ballycarbery. Father had often told them about this busy sea port with its fishing boats. The streets of the town were thronged. Maybe it was a market day! Hordes of filthy beggars roamed the streets, but also the normal business was taking place. Two or three crowded carriages passed. A group had formed outside a general store. There did not seem to be much sign of shortage here. Ladies and young girls made their way into the draper's store, the window festooned with bales of cotton and ribbon and two or three hatstands with gaily trimmed bonnets. Down a.wide lane and back behind the shops, a herd of cattle and about twenty sheep ,were being auctioned. Michael ran up the lane and walked among them. He could not believe it.

Suddenly a great hullabaloo broke out in the main square as five carts slowly approached one after the other in a line. The wooden carts creaked with the heavy weight of their load. They were laden with sacks of grain! Six soldiers appeared out of nowhere and positioned themselves on either side of the caravan as it wound its way forward.

The beggars and passersby seemed to swell in numbers and came together joining forces. The children were swallowed up in the middle of them all. They were all starving people, tired and brokenhearted, who had lost everything. The carts made their .way through the street, the horses whinnying nervously, their drivers muttering under their breath. They turned off the main square and took a street that sloped gradually downwards. The crowd, silent and jostling, still followed. One of the horses slipped but managed to right itself. Peggy clung tightly to Eily's hand, sure that something bad was about to happen.

The three children gasped when they reached the end of the street, as right in front of them stretched the harbour. Two boats were tied to the quayside and they moved very gently on the water. A large warehouse lay on one side and from this men were rolling large kegs and barrels to be placed on the boats. Two or three big muscular men had come over to the carts and begun to unload the grain. A ripple ran through the crowd that now lined the water's edge.

One old man got up his courage. 'Where is that grain being shipped to?' he asked.

'England,' was the curt reply.

The old man, whose body was bent and twisted, shook his head sadly from side to side. The crowd began to whisper, and all the time the carts were being unloaded. Two, now empty, moved off in another direction.

A tall red-haired man moved to the front of the crowd. He had a big frame but his muscles had wasted away, so there was little strength in him now.

'Stop this folly,' he shouted. 'Are ye blind? Can't you see the starving folk all around you?'

No one answered. The men kept working and the soldiers grouped themselves together. Another cart was empty by now.

'We're starving, the hunger is on us,' shouted the tall man again, unable to hide the tears in his eyes. At once about twenty other voices joined in, until they all shouted in unison, 'The hunger is on us.'

The soldier in charge stepped forward. 'Disperse. Let there be no trouble. These goods are sold and paid for.'

'We're Irishmen, and our food is being sent away, grown in Irish soil to feed English bellies, while ours are empty and our people starve and die,' the red-haired man began. 'We'll not stand for it.'

He stepped forward to try to reach a sack of grain, but one of the soldiers gave him a blow and knocked him to the ground. A gasp of dismay came from the crowd.

Then, how it happened Eily did not know, but two or three skeleton-like young men had jumped on to the carts and slashed open the sacks. At first the grain started to trickle and then it flowed out all over the cobbles below. The soldiers were trying to pull the horses into the warehouse as well as beat back some of the crowd. The children filled their fists with grain and stuffed it in their pockets and in the bag, quick as lightning, and then took to their heels and ran for their lives, not wanting to see what would happen. People were running and scattering in all directions.

'Eily, what will we do?' questioned Michael. 'I don't like this place, it's too dangerous. Let's leave it.'

Eily and Peggy agreed with him, so the children made their way out of the town. They had not gone very far when they met a farmer herding a few sheep along the road. He looked at them with suspicion.

'Excuse me, sir,' begged Michael. 'Do you know of the town of Castletaggart? Are we heading in the right direction?'

The farmer stopped and stared at them. They looked wretched and wild, but they were only children, about the same age as his own brood at home.

'Well, you are on the right path. Follow this coast road for a few miles – you'll be in view of the sea the whole time – then around the mountain and cross-country and to another main road, and that will lead you to it. It's a fair distance. Ask as you go.' He went to move off and then stopped and drew from his pocket a small loaf of bread and a large wedge of cheese. 'Here you go,' he shouted as he threw it to Michael, who just managed to catch it.

The children stood in total disbelief. Maybe their luck was changing. They had a little grain, still a few turnips left, some bread and cheese and now they knew they were near the journey's end.

They climbed over a stone wall. A lush green field sloped almost the whole way down to the sea. They had never been by the sea before and wanted to see it close up, so they walked towards it through the long grass. The view was deceptive, as the bottom of the field revealed a sheer drop down a jagged steep cliff to the lapping waves below. The children breathed in the fresh sea air, almost able to smell and taste its saltiness. They could never have imagined such vastness. Where the sea ended, the sky began. Far in the distance, a blur, which must have been a boat, could be spotted.

They found a good place to sit and rest and watch the seagulls glide in the air and circle and disappear near the cliff. They watched the cormorants dive under the water and re-emerge with a fish. The air was still and warm. Michael divided up the bread and cheese. They had forgotten how long it was since they had eaten fresh bread. Eily remembered Mother baking it – the smell would fill the cottage, and the three of them wouldn't even leave it to cool before they would wolf it down. She felt such a pang of homesickness here, in this strange place, that she had to pretend to look out to sea so the others wouldn't notice the tears in her eyes. Then they spread out a blanket and lay back, and the distant lapping of the waves soon lulled them to sleep.

When they woke they breathed a few deep breaths of sea air again and made their way back through the field and on to the dusty road.

CHAPTER 11

Travelling by Night

THE DRY SPELL CONTINUED. The sun beat down mercilessly. At midday the children would find shade under a tree and rest for about three hours. At times the road, which was now hardbaked, almost burned the soles of their feet. Little bluetits and sparrows chattered in the dust, looking for water. All the little brooks and streams had dried up, and the children's water can was empty. The shame of it was that in the distance they could still see the rippling blue of the sea mocking them. But they had heard tell that if you drank salt water it would drive you crazy. They chewed grass and pulled unripe blackberries from the brambles, desperate for moisture. They sucked stems – anything to ease the thirst. Their lips were dry, cracked and sore. This was worse than the hunger.

Rounding a bend in the road, they stopped and stared in amazement at the landscape ahead. Everything in sight was charred and blackened. Here and there tiny spirals of smoke still drifted upwards. There wasn't a blade of grass to be seen.

The children blessed themselves. The smell of burning assaulted their senses. They tied rags around their noses and mouths.

'Someone must have set a fire and not put it out,' said Michael. 'With the dry spell it just ran in all directions.'

Nothing stirred in this bleakness, not a bird or an insect or a bee or an animal. It was too quiet. Fields of what had been gorse and heather and pasture had been laid bare.

'Are we in hell?' asked Peggy, her thin little face drawn and worried.

'No,' said Eily, 'just a place destroyed. Come on, we'll move through this as quick as we can.'

Gradually colour returned to the terrain and they were surrounded by fields of long, overgrown grass, dried out and standing tall. Peggy had found a ladybird and held it gently in the palm of her hand, chatting to it. Looking at her, Eily realised how young she was, just barely seven, and how brave a little girl she was. There was no point in stopping, they just had to keep going and get to some water. Eventually they found a ditch. Large weeds and brambles grew over it and protected it from the sun's sharp rays. They knelt down in the dry mud. At the base of the ditch the earth was still a dark brown and had not yet turned grey. The could not get the water into the water can as the ditch was too shallow, so they just took turns in scooping the muddy water up in their hands and sipping it. They swallowed the dirt too. The drink did not quench their thirst, but maybe it would be of some help. Exhausted, they sat down under a row of tall beech trees.

'What will we do?' wondered Eily, out loud.

Peggy was already dozing and did not hear her. Michael's eyes were beginning to close too when he mumbled, 'Why don't we walk at night instead and in the early morning when it's cooler?'

It made such sense, Eily could have kicked herself for not thinking of it sooner. That's what they would do.

The countryside took on a different shape in the dark. Luckily there was no cloud in the sky and the moon shone down brightly on them. Although weak and exhausted, they seemed to be able to

walk for a longer distance without having to stop
for a rest. There was lots of scampering and scur-
rying in the hedgerows as they passed and Peggy
edged nearer to Eily and Michael, fearful that some
strange creature would jump out and attack her.
There were many different sights and sounds all
around them. They jumped every time they heard
the screech of the night owl getting ready to hunt
and the almost silent beat of its wings as it swooped
and caught its prey. It was a time for the hunters
and they would blink in surprise when the children
came upon them, and move into the shadows.

One time they saw a large grey badger shuffling
along, and the three of them held their breath not
wishing to disturb him. About two miles further
on they came upon a vixen and her cubs playing
outside their den, nipping and chasing each other.
The children moved on silently.

By the following night they had lost all sight of
the sea and were near the base of the mountain. At
least they were heading in the right direction, and
if they could only manage to keep going they
would be in Castletaggart in a few days and maybe
they would find some relation who would look
after them and take them in?

The next day was oppressive. There was a

constant rasping dryness in their mouths and throats, and they could hardly get a breath of air. Nothing stirred all around them. Even the birds had stopped their twittering and singing. It was strange. The only activity the children could see was the odd butterfly lazily hovering over a bunch of wild flowers. That night they had just started to get ready to move when they became aware of a low rumble in the distance. Terrified, they stayed where they were, pulling the blankets around them.

CHAPTER 12

The Thunderstorm

THE RUMBLING GREW AND GREW, getting nearer and nearer. A streak of light would flash across the orange and grey sky, then the sky itself would thunder and roar. They had never seen such a bad thunderstorm. The lightning flashes got longer and wider, stretching even from the top of the mountain down to the fields below.

The children were terrified. Was it the end of the world? They prayed out loud to be spared.

Peggy was whimpering like a young puppy and had burrowed herself in between the other two, with her head hidden well under the shawl and the blankets. Eily was trying to stop herself shaking and was making a great effort to control her own fears.

The whole sky lit up every few minutes as the

sheets of lightning flared all around them. The thunder was deafening. It was as if the huge clouds were banging into each other and fighting. Never in all their young lives had they seen or heard anything like it. Sometimes it would stop for a few minutes but then – Crash! – with a rumble it would all be back and start up again.

After a while, Michael relaxed a bit and began to make jokes about two huge giants fighting and trying to kill each other, up in a land above the clouds.

'You take that,' he'd shout when the thunder rolled. 'I'll strike you with my sword,' when the lightning flashed.

On and on went the fighting for hours on end, and even Peggy, the odd time, would add on a bit to the story, but she would not stick her head out to have a look at what was going on.

Then, as suddenly as it had started, the thunder and noise seemed to ease off and stop, though they could hear it in the distance.

Eily felt a droplet of rain on her nose, then another, and all at once the heavens opened. The rain came in torrents, beating down on them, and within a few seconds they were absolutely drenched. The water fell with such force that it stung them. It was almost like being attacked by a swarm of insects. They fought to catch their breath. They opened their mouths, gulping the droplets down. The hard earth and dust underfoot softened and gradually became muddy.

Every living thing, although battered, seemed to stretch to absorb the much needed wet and moisture. Life was being renewed. The brooks and streams and rivers would fill again and flow through the countryside.

Michael threw off the blanket and danced around with pure joy in the early morning light, splattering himself with mud which the rain sluiced off him. The water cans filled up quickly.

Within a few hours the rain had stopped, the sun was up and bright, but without the harshness and glare of the previous few days. Now they could walk by day again.

CHAPTER 13

Peggy's Fever

EILY COULD NOT UNDERSTAND IT. The past two days had been perfect – they had had their fill to drink, a portion of grain each to chew. She had found a clump of large plump strawberries and also some tiny little hazelnuts. But Peggy was constantly cranky and whingeing and lagging behind. Michael and Eily took it in turns to catch her by her good arm and pull her along. She kept wanting to sit and rest. She was hungry and thin and exhausted, but so were they all.

Once or twice in frustration Eily had given her a wallop on the bottom, now knowing how Mother must have felt when they had been bold. However, Peggy would invariably break into tears and sit down. Eily tried to keep calm and remember all the good things about Peggy. Michael constantly teased her, which was his way of dealing with the annoyance. They had passed the side of the mountain, and when they had got across country for another bit more they would find themselves on the road to Castletaggart – nearly at the end of their journey. Eily was letting herself drift into a dream where they were re-united with Mother and Father and had gone back to the old cottage and all the neighbours were there to greet them and …

'Eily! Eily! Quick, it's Peggy!' shouted Michael.

She jerked out of her dream and ran back through the coarse grass.

'What's wrong with that child now?' she muttered angrily. 'I suppose she's sitting down for another little rest …' She stopped her sharp words. Peggy was lying on the ground, her eyes shut and her breathing coming too quickly. They both stood over her.

'Peggy! Peggy!'

Peggy did not move or stir.

'Oh my God, what is it?' cried Eily, kneeling down. She touched Peggy's forehead. It was burning. The skin on her shoulders and legs and everywhere was hot to touch. She was burning up with a fever.

Michael ran on ahead to search for somewhere that would give a bit of shelter. A large hawthorn tree stood in the middle of the long coarse grass. Near the side of the field, about two yards from it, grew a few bushy shrubs. It was well hidden and protected. Michael came back up to Eily. They could not rouse Peggy. They laid a blanket on the ground and gently rolled her on to it, and then between the two of them they half-dragged and half-lifted it under the tree.

Peggy did not seem to be aware of what was going on around her. Eily settled her and placed the other blanket over her. A huge wave of guilt washed over Eily. She should have noticed that Peggy was sickening for something. She was meant to be the oldest and wisest – 'the little Mother'!

'Do you think she has the fever, Eily?' asked Michael. 'Or is it something after the dog biting her arm?'

Eily shook her head. 'I don't know, Michael, but whatever it is she's burning up and very sick. It must have been coming on for the past few days.'

Then she remembered Mary Kate's medicine and got the jar and mixed some of the powder with water. She raised Peggy a bit and managed to pour some of it into her mouth. Peggy spluttered as it went down her throat, and then seemed to sink back into a long deep sleep.

'Will we light a fire?' questioned Michael, trying to think of something to help the situation. He set about looking for flint stones and gathered any pieces of dry twigs and moss that he could find. He preferred to be busy. He did not want to have time to think or worry.

Eily watched him. Then for an hour he tried to get a spark to light the fire, but nothing happened. Eily had a few goes too.

'Leave it, Michael, we can try later.' Eily dampened a cloth with water and laid it to Peggy's burning cheeks and forehead. Her whole head of dark brown hair was clammy with sweat as she tossed and turned. A few times she called out for Mother in a low voice.

'Hush, love. Hush, love,' was all that Eily could manage.

All that day and night Eily sat with Peggy, stroking her hair and holding her hand, giving her the fever mixture and trying to cool her down. Michael went off in search of nettles and roots and herbs to mix with a bit of water to make a thin cold soup. At night Michael dozed off, but Eily forced herself to stay awake. The little girl tossed and turned and sometimes cried out in pain. She had a nightmare about the dogs attacking her, and kept shouting 'Dog, the dog,' her eyes wide and staring, before collapsing back into a heavy sleep. Eily knew that Peggy didn't know who she was with or where she was. Also she couldn't help wondering, would they all get the fever now. Who would look after her if she got sick? She could feel her head bursting with the worry of it all. Eily kept checking Peggy's skin. It was burning like fire with no sign of cooling down. However, there was no tinge of yellow to it at all. That was a good sign. Her skin glowed pink with her temperature and her two cheeks were a rosy red.

As she dozed lightly, Eily thought about Mother and Bridget, the baby nestled into her arms. Had Mother gone to join her little one in heaven? Eily opened her heart and prayed, 'Don't let Peggy die – don't take away my little sister – keep her safe – let her get well.'

Eily dozed and when she woke up the early morning was damp. Her arms and back were stiff and sore. Peggy was still in a deep sleep, her breathing loud and far too fast.

Eily walked away a few yards to relieve herself and then took the can of water and gulped some down; the rest she splashed on her face and back to try and wake herself up. She could send Michael for more when he roused himself. If only they had the fire. She picked up the flints, sparking them off each other in a temper. It caught some dried moss and began to smoulder! She hardly dared move as she angled a few twigs to catch the small flame. They were a bit damp and cold after the night and spluttered a little, but they took. Now at least they had the comfort of a bit of fire.

Michael and Eily both felt useless. There was very little they could do but sit and stay near Peggy. Michael roved around frantically to find something of substance to eat, but to no avail. Flower heads, grass, leaves, everything was being added to the water along with a tiny bit of grain, but it did nothing to kill the growing hunger pains in their stomachs. Michael kept his eyes constantly peeled for the sight of a rabbit or hare but never saw even the sign of one. It was hopeless. Soon both of them would be too weak to walk. They would have to do something.

Michael disappeared for the morning with a grim look on his face, and came back with some kind of creature skinned and cleaned out, but there was little eating in it. Cooked with the nettle leaves, it was disgusting, and a feeling of queasiness washed over Eily as she forced herself to swallow it and later to try and keep it down.

That evening, with Peggy's head resting in her lap, Eily couldn't help but wonder what would have happened if they had gone to the workhouse with Tom Daly and the crowd from their district. Peggy wouldn't be sick, and they might have had a bit of stew and a piece of bread each day. Had she made the wrong choice and cost them all their lives? She felt so depressed and downhearted. Maybe they could still go to a workhouse. There was bound to be one somewhere around. They might get help there. The idea burned in her brain. She couldn't leave Peggy, but Michael – he could go, maybe, and someone might come to help them with Peggy.

CHAPTER 14

Michael's Desperate Search

MICHAEL SET OFF ACROSS THE FIELDS. He had stock-piled enough fuel to keep the fire going. He felt frightened and strange on his own, but knew that Eily should stay with Peggy. Eily had hugged him close when he was leaving, and further on he turned back for a last look, wondering would he ever see his two sisters again. He knew basically which direction to take. He hoped he might meet someone along the road who would tell him the way to the workhouse.

He walked for over an hour and a half without seeing a sinner, then at the end of a small boreen he noticed a curl of smoke coming from a broken-down old cabin. He made his way to it and hammered against the door. No one replied. He remembered the trick he had played when they were left on their own in the cottage and how scared they had been.

'I don't want to come in, don't worry. I just want directions. Is the town of Castletaggart anywhere near here?'

There was no reply, so he repeated the question.

A deep husky voice answered. 'It's a good two to three days' walk for tired legs and feet.'

'Is there a workhouse roundabouts, then?' begged Michael.

The old man inside considered before he spoke. 'I heard that the O'Leary mill had been turned into a workhouse. It's about a half-day from here. You keep to the main road and turn off at the bridge over the running river, then right, and you can't help but see it.' Then, as an afterthought, the voice added, 'But I'd prefer to die in my own bed and not with strangers.'

'Thank you,' said Michael, starting to move off.

'God spare you, lad, and keep you from all harm.'

Michael felt sad for the old man all alone in the world with no one to look after him.

He kept walking on. Two or three times he felt dizzy and lightheaded and had to sit down to get his breath back. He could hear the river water running, but still could not see it. Then up ahead he was able to make out the crossroads and the humpy bridge. Two women lay on the ground near the bridge. They were both so weak they didn't notice the young boy pass them.

Michael could not believe it when he came to the old mill. Crowds of people were waiting, sleeping on the cobblestones. They could go no further. A few of them were grouped together in families. They lay in their rags or blankets, relieved not to be on their own. From within the building came a constant moaning and crying, and a smell of disease and sickness seemed to fill the air around the place. Some people were praying out loud.

A nun, dressed in full habit, came through a small wooden door. She spoke in a loud voice: 'This place is full. We have no space for man, woman or child, nor is there spare food. Perhaps by tomorrow when we have removed those who have died of sickness and the fever, we may be able to take a few.'

A murmur ran through the crowd and the women began to wail and cry. They had no place left to go, here was as good a place to die as any-where else. At least they might get a blessing said over them.

Michael began to run – he did not know where the energy came from – down past the bridge and back the way he had come. Tears coursed down his face. He could feel a pain in his chest and knew that his heart was broken in two and his childhood gone forever. He slowed down, he had a long and miser-able way to go. There was no God, and if there was he was a monster.

Eily kept watching Peggy. She thrashed and moaned and cried for Mother again and again. Eily gave her more of the medicine and couldn't help but notice that the jar was nearly empty. She herself was exhausted too. Nothing she could say or do would help Peggy now. She put her arms around her and kissed her little button nose and the freck-les on her cheeks. The skin felt cooler to the touch. Within half an hour Peggy was freezing. Despite an extra blanket, shivers ran though her body and her teeth chattered.

Eily got in under the blankets with her, trying to keep her warm. The day itself was bright and sunny with just a soft breeze blowing. Eily hugged her close. She was only the weight of a baby. Eily rubbed each limb, trying to still the shivering and shaking.

'I'm here, Peggy. I'm here, Peggy,' she kept whispering, not sure if her little sister could even hear her.

At last the shivering and chattering teeth began to still. Peggy's body seemed more relaxed, her breathing quieter. She slept in the comfort of Eily's arms, her head on her chest.

Eily looked up through the hawthorn tree. Its heavy branches moved softly in the breeze, the blue sky peeping through. Eily thought she noticed a blackbird up above, hiding among the foliage. Her eyes felt heavy and before she knew it, she was asleep.

Michael walked slowly. There was no rush now that he had nothing to bring back. He crossed a low broken-down stone wall. He could smell some wild garlic, and he rooted until he found it and put some in his pocket. One more wall and field to cross before he would be safely back with the girls.

Gradually Michael became aware of the sound

of mooing. A cow had tried to get in over a ditch and her two legs had got caught in a large pile of brambles and thorns. They were embedded into her pale brown-and-white skin. Michael hated to see an animal in distress or pain and his first instinct was to help. He had passed a field with about twenty cows in it over a mile back and noticed the cowherd asleep on the grass. This cow must have strayed from there. Suddenly he got an idea. He took to his heels and ran, hell for leather.

'Eily! Eily! Get up, quick. Come on, we've no time to lose,' Michael shouted.

Eily stretched. Peggy was snoring gently. She lowered Peggy's head down on the blanket. She rubbed her eyes. The sun was going down. It was nearly dusk. She must have been asleep for hours.

'Eily, will you come on. We only have a bit of a chance. Get the blade and the water can.' He had already begun to run back through the weeds and grass.

Eily dropped a few twigs on the fire which had nearly gone out, picked up the blade and can and followed him.

CHAPTER 15

The Cow

'WAIT, MICHAEL! WHAT IS IT? Where are we going?' she shouted.

He turned back and signalled her to be quiet. Within a minute he had led her to the ditch where the cow stood, still trapped.

Eily looked puzzled. Surely he wasn't going to try and kill the cow. She patted her on the rump. The cow looked around balefully, her liquid brown eyes soft and gentle but yet afraid.

'Keep a look-out for a minute,' urged Michael.

She let her eyes roam around but couldn't see anything move.

'What are you going to do?' she hissed.

'I'm going to bleed her,' he replied.

'What?' said Eily. 'But you don't know how to, Michael.'

'I heard Father tell us stories often enough about times before the potatoes failed and he and his father bled the landlord's cattle. Come here and give me a hand.'

He was patting the cow on the neck and rubbing his hand down her front and side to find a vein. His father had told him that if you hit the main vein by mistake, the animal would bleed to death in a few minutes. He searched around until he found a likely one. Eily passed him the blade. He made a nick in the finer skin under the neck, but nothing happened. He deepened the cut and a droplet or two of blood appeared. The cow lowed and rolled her frightened eyes.

'Easy girl, easy,' assured Eily, patting her and trying to calm her. Michael was squeezing at the opening with his fingers. The blood began to trickle and then to flow freely and spatter on the ground. Eily held the can to catch it as it fell. The blood seemed to pump quicker and quicker and in a little while the can was nearly full. Michael then made Eily put pressure on the vein and hold it to stop the bleeding while he mixed a paste of clay and grass and spit and smeared it on the cut. It took about ten minutes before it slowed down to a slight seepage. The animal was baffled. They helped to tear the brambles and thorns from her legs and pull her out of the ditch, and then they led her back into the field. Michael knew it would only be a matter of time before the cowherd would come searching for her.

They couldn't believe it when, about five minutes later, they heard the young man calling the cow. Although they were a good distance away, they were terrified and lay down in the long grass, hoping they were well hidden. Eily kept a good hold of the precious can. They did not dare to stir for about twenty minutes, then they got back to Peggy as quickly as they could.

She was still dozing peacefully. Her skin and temperature felt more normal to the touch.

'Well, Michael, what about the workhouse? Is it far? Will we be able to get help for Peggy?' Eily kept on with a barrage of questions.

Michael hardly knew where to begin. He bowed his head, avoiding her eyes.

'Things are desperate,' he whispered. Eily got down on her knees, and touched his arm. 'The

workhouse is a few hours'. walk,' he continued.
'We'd never manage to carry her that far, and
anyway it would be no good.' He stopped for a
moment. 'Eily, it was dreadful. You could hear the
crying and moaning from down the road – and the
smell! It's a place of sickness. Outside, the people
sit, waiting for a bed to die on. They're all like
corpses but still alive, just about. And food –
there's none, divil a bit. We have no place to go.
Castletaggart is still a two- or three-day walk.
We're too weak – we'd never make it. My head is
giddy and light. Maybe we should just lie here and
wait?'

'What about the can? We've got that now. That's
something,' pleaded Eily. 'It'll give us a bit of
strength.'

She got up, took the can and poured enough
from it to cover the base of the pot. If only they had
a bit of meal or something to mix into it. There were
a few bits of grain and husks down at the bottom
of the bag. She emptied them in. Michael silently
handed her a bit of the wild garlic and she added
part of it to the mixture and then held it over the
low fire. She took care that the mixture didn't burn
as it thickened and stuck together, making a dark
brown, nearly black cake. She divided it up, giving

Michael the largest portion.

The taste was strange and strong. She nibbled at hers and then swallowed it quickly, as it was a bit crumbly. She had reserved a piece, just in case, for Peggy. They were both exhausted and spent the evening resting. Michael fell asleep, at one stage crying out as though in a nightmare.

Then, as if a miracle had happened, Peggy opened her eyes.

'Eily, can I have a sup of water? I'm really thirsty.'

She was totally baffled by Eily's cries of joy and endearments. The little girl drank a full can of water. Her face was as pale as snow and her eyes were like two huge brown dots with deep circles underneath. Eily took her up on her lap and kissed her nearly from top to toe. Her fever was gone. She would get better now. Eily sang her a few of her favourite songs and kept telling her what a good little girl she was.

Michael was just as surprised when he woke at mid-morning and found Peggy sitting up, leaning against the curved tree trunk. He gave her a wink, then ran across the field and picked an assortment of wild flowers and dropped them on her lap. The little girl was flattered with all the attention. She felt shaky and weak, but had no memory of how sick she had been. Eily gave her the left-over blood cake from the night before. She would make more that evening. After a while, Peggy dozed off again.

Michael and Eily decided that they must get Peggy and themselves strong enough again for the rest of the journey. It was their only chance.

The next few days were spent hunting for food. They had to keep the fire going also. They had finished the blood. Michael went searching at night and had been lucky enough to catch a rat and a hedgehog. They had lost their squeamishness by now and knew that all that mattered was their survival. Nettles were plentiful, and every ripening berry was also picked.

At last Peggy was back on her feet. On the third day, Michael and Eily got her to the stream. She sat on a rock as Eily washed her, and afterwards her skin tingled and she felt the last trace of the sickness had been washed away.

By midday the breeze had freshened. The sky had darkened and clouds scudded along, blocking out the sun.

'Will we make a start?' questioned Eily. 'Do you think you're ready yet, Peggy?'

A bit of colour had started to creep back into the

little girl's wan features.

'I want to go and find the aunts, the ones that made the beautiful cake for Mother,' answered Peggy.

They collected their stuff and threw dirt on the fire. It looked like it might start to drizzle soon and it would be best to get on the way once more.

CHAPTER 16

Castletaggart

NO WONDER FINE LADIES drive around in carriages, thought Eily. Walking is only for the poor! The walk seemed so long. She had fallen into step with Peggy, who could not be hurried or pushed too far. They all kept their heads down and did not speak, everyone wrapped deep in their own thoughts.

They passed a field of cows, and Michael and Eily smiled, wondering if their cow-friend remembered them. Michael had also pointed out the turn at the crossroads that led to the workhouse.

They took the journey slowly, walking along the road, sitting down for frequent rests.

One time they were sitting against a high demesne wall. Like a fortress it guarded the land and gardens and leafy walks of an old estate. The grand house with its broad stone steps and magnificent flower beds and garden ornaments was hidden from prying eyes. Peggy was engrossed watching an army of ants as they marched back and forth, disappearing into a small hole in the dusty brick.

'Look what's behind the wall,' she called to her older brother and sister. But they ignored her. 'Look, Eily, they've got apples and bushes of berries.'

Eily ran over and looked through the crack. She let out a gasp. But the wall was too high – it was about twenty feet tall, designed to keep people out. Michael walked around the front section of the wall to see if at any stage it dipped or a branch of a tree leaned over it.

Suddenly Peggy was jumping up and down with excitement and pointing to a section of wall that seemed to be cracked. Long grass reached up and behind it and ivy had taken root and spread the whole way up to the top. Peggy pulled back the ivy to reveal a small gap where two or three blocks of stone had crumbled and worn away. They would never fit through it.

'I'll be able to squeeze through,' boasted Peggy. 'After all, I'm the littlest one.'

Eily knew it was stealing, but these times were different. She handed Peggy the near-empty food bag.

'Promise me, Peggy, if you hear anything you'll get out straight away,' said Eily solemnly. Peggy just nodded her head and disappeared through the ivy.

Eily moved further up along the wall trying to peep through a narrow crack. She couldn't see Peggy at all. It seemed like the little one was in there for an age. Michael was anxiously pacing up and down outside. Suddenly Peggy's dark hair peeped through the ivy and she passed a bulging bag out to Michael. She dipped back in and then climbed out clutching a fistful of multicoloured stems of gladioli and heavy waxen peonies. Eily had to stop herself from laughing.

They walked about a quarter of a mile down the road, then climbed up over a stile and sat down to eat, hidden from the road behind a pile of brambles.

'Oh, Eily, you should have seen the place,' yearned Peggy. 'There were all kinds of berries and fruits there.' The bag was jammed with an assortment of gooseberries, raspberries, huge strawberries and some windfall apples that were still very hard and green. 'There was a little white seat to sit on, and a thing in the centre of a little pond with water spurting out of its mouth, and little fishes swimming all around. I would have tried to catch one, but they were very small and all goldy colour. There was another huge wall inside and there was a white gate in the middle of it, but it was locked and when I looked through the gate there was a whole field, full of cabbages and caulies and carrots and onions and big things of corn and huge marrows. Oh, if only the gate had been open.'

'You did really well, pet,' reassured Eily, as they all dipped in their hands and filled them with the berries. What sweetness and juiciness filled their mouths! Peggy insisted on carrying the bunch of flowers, saying they were for the aunts.

The next morning they all had cramps in their stomachs and chewed Mary Kate's special remedy, hoping it would give them some relief.

A priest passed by with his little horse and trap. They asked him if it was much further to Castletaggart. He held his handkerchief to his face when he turned to answer them. They would be there by six o'clock, he assured them, and then he jiggled the horse's reins and went off in the same direction, not even offering them a lift.

Peggy started to cry. 'We'll never get there – it's too far – my legs ache.'

Eily bent down and massaged her leg muscles. 'Maybe they're growing pains, pet, now you're getting to be such a big girl,' she encouraged. Michael offered to carry the drooping bundle of flowers for her.

Every step seemed like ten steps as they travelled the rest of their journey, willing themselves to reach the town. It was nearly nightfall when they got there. Castletaggart at last! Peggy's mouth hung open with wonder and Michael tried to walk tall and straight and proud.

'Look at the buildings! Look at the shops!' shouted Peggy, pointing in every direction.

Although the three of them were bone-weary and exhausted and it was almost dark, a sense of excitement rushed through their veins.

'Where's the shop? Where are the aunties?' Peggy kept pestering Eily.

To Eily it was like a dream come true. A wide grin spread across her face. She had done it, she had got them all safely here. They were weak, but they were in Castletaggart. They walked through the town.

One or two people brushed past them, unwilling

to meet their gaze, afraid of being asked for help. The place was quiet and the streets were nearly empty. A few men sat inside the doors of two pubs, supping porter.

A high white building stood on the left-hand side of the street. Large steps led up to it and men and women chatted outside its doors. One huge room was lit by a chandelier and tables were set, ready for dinner.

A soldier stopped when he saw the children and came over. 'Come on, you brats, move away from the hotel. We want no beggars in this town. What's your business here?'

Eily felt herself go crimson, suddenly aware of how badly they looked. 'We're looking for our aunts – they have a shop here,' she told him.

The soldier stared at them in disbelief. 'What kind of a shop would this be?' he questioned.

'One with cakes and tarts and pies,' piped up Peggy.

The soldier scratched his head at such a notion but eventually pointed them towards a side street.

Eily could not believe it – finally here. Her heart was hammering in her chest. They walked down the street, passing houses that opened right on to it. The soldier had said the shop had a blue and white door, and a big wide blue window with white shutters. At last they found it! The blinds were drawn. The children tapped at the door, but no one came. They lifted the knocker – no one was at home. Maybe the aunts had gone out? They slipped down a narrow alleyway and lay down to sleep.

Tomorrow, they would try again.

CHAPTER 17

Journey's End

THE SOUNDS OF THE TOWN woke the children. They stretched. All their muscles were stiff and sore. Eily brushed the loose dust and dirt from their clothes. Inside, she was bursting with hope and almost felt light-hearted. Today was the day. They had made it. They were right in the middle of Castletaggart. This was the town their Mother had so often talked about.

They walked the short distance back towards the shop. Storekeepers were already setting out their wares and putting up stands with their selection of goods on display. The owner of the hardware store hung buckets and pots and pans and jugs from brass hooks around his shopfront. Shovels and fire-irons lay stacked near the door. Peggy was so amazed at all the goings-on that she walked straight into a pile of green watering cans and sent them flying.

The children stared longingly at the provisions store, their eyes transfixed by the amount of food there. Sacks of flour and meal lay heavily under the counter. From the ceiling hung large hunks of various meats. On a painted white shelf were jars of various sweets. The shopkeeper was carefully wiping some freshly laid eggs and placing them in a wicker basket, while his wife was weighing out small bags of tea. The children swallowed hard, realising just how hungry they really were.

Eily pulled Peggy by the hand and moved quickly towards the shop with the blue and white shutters. A woman was standing outside with a bucket of water and a mop. She wore a large white apron.

Peggy was nearly bursting with excitement. 'Is that one of Mammy's aunties?' she whispered.

Eily wasn't sure, and cautiously approached the woman, who was busy washing down the front door step and the path outside the shop. The woman turned and caught sight of them.

'Get away out of it, ye spalpeens. There's nothing for ye here. Go on, now, or I'll call the soldiers.'

'We're Eily and Michael and Peggy O'Driscoll,' began Eily, 'Margaret Murphy from Drumneagh's children.'

The woman stared at them. 'Divil a bit do I care who you are. I don't know ye, anyways. Move on, now, it should be the workhouse or the roads for the likes of ye.' Eily's heart sank.

Peggy stood staring straight ahead. Huge tears filled her eyes. 'You're not our auntie.'

The woman shook her head, and turned around and began to wash with the mop, ignoring them. Eily went back up to her again.

'Mam, did ye ever hear of the Murphys of Drumneagh – Nano and Lena were our grandmother's sisters. They would be quite old now. They had a shop, a baking shop. Did you ever hear tell of them?'

The woman set aside her broom, then walked to the corner of the street and pointed to the far end of the main street.

'There's a lane over there that runs off the market square. It's called Market Lane. There used to be a shop there run by two old ladies. Try there.'

Then she turned on her heel and walked back, not wanting to entertain one more word of conver-

sation with them. She picked up the bucket and
mop and closed the door firmly behind her.

The children stood still. The town was beginning
to fill up. They crossed the street and found Market
Lane. They walked up and down it twice. There
was no sign of the aunts' shop. There were stables
and a closed-up general store – and then beside it
they noticed a house with a small bay window. The
paint was peeling and the doorway was dirty. It
could have been a shop!

Eily went to knock at the door and was surprised
when it opened. They edged their way into a
gloomy room, divided by a wooden counter. On a
shelf behind, dusty rows of jams and preserves
stood to attention. This couldn't be the place,
thought Eily. Not the clean busy shop, packed with
customers on market day. A wave of disappointment rushed over her.

Peggy's eyes were popping out of her head as
she looked around. 'There's no cakes or pies here.
Where are they?'

Eily tried to shush her. An old woman appeared
from behind a heavy drape at the far side of the
counter. She was stooped and moved slowly. Her
white hair was tied up in a neat bun. She blessed
herself when she saw the children.

'Ye poor starved craters, I've nothing for you here. Go up the town and you might have a better chance of a bit of help,' she said kindly. 'Where are your mother and father to be letting you roam around all alone?'

'Auntie Lena,' said Eily, her voice trembling.

The old woman stopped. She stared at the children. Walking skeletons, not a pick on any of them. The boy was filthy and the little one looked as if a puff of wind would nearly knock her over. And the older girl, she looked worn-out. The old lady shook her head. Imagine having to live through these desperate times.

'Auntie Lena,' repeated Eily, 'you're our grand-aunt. We're Margaret and John O'Driscoll's children. I'm Eily and this is Michael and this is our little sister Peggy.'

The old lady stood staring at them open-mouthed. She pulled up a chair and sat down. She gazed at them. The older girl was like Margaret, her mother. But they looked like beggars, or children from the workhouse.

'I am Lena Murphy,' she answered.

'Where's the other one?' piped up Peggy.

'Oh, do you mean my sister Nano? She's up in bed. She's not very strong and has to rest a lot.'

Peggy edged her way forward and handed the drooping dirty bunch of flowers to her grandaunt. Lena could not help smiling.

'I've never had a cake with icing on the top and sugar violets,' confided Peggy.

The old lady looked at them. It was just unbelievable that these urchins were related to her. They looked famished and exhausted. They must have walked a very long way.

She brought them through to the kitchen and sat them down. She set the kettle to boil and got out fresh soda bread and a jar of her best plum jam. There would be time enough for the story of what had happened, and where Margaret and John were, but the first thing was to get a bit inside them before they passed out. From upstairs came a knocking on the floor.

That sister of mine, Nano, is always looking for something, thought Lena to herself. Well, Nano Murphy, you are in for a shock when you find out just who is sitting in our back kitchen, and the story they have to tell!

Eily looked around her. The place was old and could do with a lick of paint, but it was clean and neat. One shelf held a row of fine delph, another, various sizes of jars and baking dishes. They were with family – that was the most important thing. She hoped above all hopes that they could stay. An angry stomping could be heard upstairs, followed by a thumping noise coming down the wooden stairs. A large round-faced woman, her grey curls hanging loose to her shoulders, stood at the bottom in a blue flannel nightgown and a grey shawl. Total disbelief came over her face when she saw the children.

'Have you lost your senses, Lena? Letting a crowd of beggars into our kitchen, and Lord knows we've little enough – next thing we'll be getting the fever. Go away out of it you young pups and don't be taking advantage of an old woman's soft heart.' Nano had said her piece.

'Will you whisht, Nano, and calm down. These are Margaret's children, Mary Ellen's grandchildren, our own flesh and blood,' said Lena sharply.

Nano came closer and peered at them. Despite their haggard appearance and under the layer of dirt – yes, there were some resemblances. She sat down with a plop on an old stuffed chair, pulling her shawl around her.

'Where have you come from? Where's Margaret?' She began to bombard them with questions.

Lena came over and scolded her. 'Let them have

a sup of tay first – can't you see, woman, that the children are all done in?'

The children sipped the hot sweet milky tea and stuffed the soda bread and jam into their mouths, finishing off the loaf. The two aunts sat and watched them, neither of them saying a word, each engrossed in her own thoughts.

When all was finished, Lena threw two extra sods on the fire. Peggy ran over and climbed on her lap, then Eily and Michael began the story – from Father going to work on the roads scheme, to baby Bridget dying and Mother going off to search for him, then their having to leave the cottage, and the kindness of Mary Kate. The beauty of the countryside and the constant search for food. The horrors along the way. Peggy's desperate illness, and the aching exhaustion of walking so far, and how they had finally come to find Market Lane. When Eily looked up, the two aunts were busily blowing their noses and drying their eyes.

'Well, dotes, none of you will take one step further as long as myself and Nano are here. We haven't much now, as you can see, but there is room enough for our own, and maybe the good Lord in time will direct Margaret or John here to find you.'

Lena had stood up and was holding her arms open to them. Eily relaxed at last, knowing they would be safe in their new home with Nano and Lena. But, at the same moment, she knew their hearts would always belong to the little thatched cottage with the flat stones outside, and the small overgrown garden, and the fields around it with the breeze blowing softly through the hawthorn tree.

A Simple History of
The Great Famine
1845-1850

IN IRELAND LONG AGO most of the people were poor, very poor. They lived and worked on land that was not their own.

Their homes were small cottages and cabins which were overcrowded and dirty. They had small plots of land beside their houses to grow their own food. The potato was grown everywhere, as it yielded the most. Their food was largely potatoes and milk, but this was enough to keep them going.

Then, in the summer of 1845 after a long wet spell, when the people went to dig their potatoes, they could not believe it – the potatoes had got a disease and were rotting in the ground. No matter what they did, the potatoes turned to sludge and slime. This disease spread all over the country to every part of Ireland.

The people prayed to God to save them. Famine had come. They were desperate. They searched for food and sold everything they had. Most went hungry.

There were plenty of other crops, but most of them were sold and exported to other countries. The poor had no money to buy food. The government had to import boatloads of Indian corn meal (yellow meal) to feed them. But this was not enough.

Within a year large public works schemes had been set up. People worked at building roads, clearing land and so on. The work was hard for those that were already under-nourished and weak, but it was a way of earning some money.

Workhouses were crowded with those who had no-where to go and nothing to eat. Life there was rigid and strict.

Some of the landlords did all they could to help their tenants, while others just ignored the situation. Worst of all were the landlords who evicted the tenants who could not pay rent and pulled down their simple cabins.

By the end of the summer of 1846 it was clear that the potato crop had failed again. The people had nothing. They roamed the country. The work schemes were totally crowded and people rioted outside the workhouses, trying to get in.

With the starvation now came disease – famine fever, typhus, dysentery. These spread among the already weakened people.

Ireland had become a land of living ghosts. Parishes could not keep up with the amount of deaths and had to open mass graves. Soup kitchens were set up, but still death and disease spread throughout the country.

The cycle kept on. During 1847 and the following years, approximately one million men, women and children set sail for Liverpool and North America. Many died on the long rough sea-voyages and those that survived had to work very hard to make a new life in a strange land.

For those at home the winter of 1847-1848 was one of the worst ever. This was followed by the potato blight in the autumn of 1848 and again in 1849. People died on the roads, in the streets, in the cottages and fields. All in all, about one million died. In a small country like Ireland it was a huge proportion of the population.

Those that emigrated to America and Canada brought with them their strength and their courage and hope. Those that were left behind struggled to survive and worked to build a country where such a disaster could never happen again.

Other books from O'Brien Press

UNDER THE HAWTHORN TREE

Marita Conlon-McKenna
A moving story set in the time of the Great Irish Famine
(1845-50). Winner of *The International Reading Association Award*.
Illustrative chapter headings, related to the story, by Donald
Teskey.
Age group: 10-14 £3.95 *Paperback*

WILDFLOWER GIRL

Marita Conlon-McKenna
Peggy, the youngest child from *Under the Hawthorn Tree*, now 13,
emigrates to America to work as a servant. A compelling and
emotional adventure.
Age group: 10-14 £4.50 *Paperback*

JULIET'S STORY

William Trevor
First children's book by this world-renowned author. Juliet loved
stories. Her friend Kitty Ann preferred to watch television. But
Juliet said that the pictures she carried away from stories were
more real and more vivid than those that flickered on the screen.
This is the story of how Juliet finds her own story.
Age group: 8-12 £6.95 *Hardback*

THE DRUID'S TUNE

Orla Melling
The characters from Celtic myths of ancient Ireland brought to life
when two teenagers become entangled in their world through a
series of time-change adventures.
Age group: 12+ £4.50 *Paperback*

WHIZZ QUIZ

Sean C. O'Leary
Chockful of quizzes (two-thirds of the book), with puzzles, tricks
and games to delight children.
Age group: 6-10 £2.99 *Paperback*

THE FIVE HUNDRED

Eilís Dillon

Luca, an ambitious antique dealer, buys his heart's desire, a Fiat 500. When his car is stolen, life becomes dangerously exciting.
Age group: 7-10 £3.95 *Paperback*

THE CRUISE OF THE SANTA MARIA

Eilís Dillon

A sailing yarn from the west coast of Ireland.
Age group: 9+ £4.50 *Paperback*

LIVING IN IMPERIAL ROME

Eilís Dillon

Life under Trajan the Emperor, 2000 years ago in Rome. All the drama of a time when gladiators fought to the death in the arena.
Age group: 10+ £4.95 *Paperback*

YOUR MOVE

A Chess Adventure for Young Beginners
Michael Fitzpatrick

A simple, amusing and entertaining introduction to the world's greatest game. Combines fiction and instruction.
Age group: 8-12 £5.95 *Hardback*

JIMEEN

A Comic Irish Classic
Pádraig O Siochfhradha – illustrated by Brian Bourke
The first English translation of the much-loved antics of this madcap character.
Age group: 9-14 £3.50 *Paperback*
£5.95 *Hardback*

THE GREAT PIG ESCAPE

Linda Moller

Thirteen pigs make a bid for freedom and a better life. Will they be caught? Or will they be free forever...?
Age group: 8-10 £3.95 *Paperback*

BRIAN BORU

Emperor of the Irish
Morgan Llywelyn
The story of Brian Boru's exciting career – it brings the High King and tenth-century Ireland to life for young readers as never before.
Age group: 10-14 £3.95 *Paperback*

BIKE HUNT

A Story of Thieves and Kidnappers
Hugh Galt
An exciting story, set in Dublin and county Wicklow – winner of the Young People's Books medal in the Irish Book Awards.
Age group: 10-14 £3.95 *Paperback*

CYRIL

The Tale of an Orphaned Squirrel
Eugene McCabe
A moving story set in nature – winner of the Reading Association Award.
Age group: 8-11 £3.95 *Paperback*

THE LUCKY BAG

Classic Irish Children's Stories
Ed. Eilís Dillon, Pat Donlon, Pat Egan and Peter Fallon
A collection of the best in Irish children's literature.
Age group: 10-14 £4.95 *Paperback*

THE LOST ISLAND

Eilís Dillon
The mystery and danger of the sea in this gripping adventure story.
Age group: 10-14 £3.95 *Paperback*

FAERY NIGHTS / OÍCHEANTA SÍ

Micheál Mac Liammóir
A unique treasury of Celtic stories in dual language texts, illustrated by the author
Age group: 7-10 £3.50 *Paperback*

THE LITTLE BLACK SHEEP

Written and illustrated by Elizabeth Shaw
A simple, charming book to delight the younger child.
Age group: 5-7 £3.95 *Hardback*

THE COOL MAC COOL

Gordon Snell – illustrated by Wendy Shea
The life and times of legendary Celtic hero Finn MacCool
Age group: 9+ £4.95 *Paperback*

ZANY TALES

Pat Ingoldsby
A collection of hilarious off-the-wall tales for younger children.
Age group: 5-7 £3.95 *Paperback*

EXPLORING THE BOOK OF KELLS

George Otto Simms
A world-renowned authority offers a compact guide to an outstanding national treasure. £6.95 *Hardback*

BRENDAN THE NAVIGATOR

Explorer of the Ancient World
George Otto Simms
One of the great adventures of the world, made famous by Tim Severin.
£3.95 *Paperback*
£6.95 *Hardback*

THE TAIN

Liam MacUistin
The great heroic and romantic Celtic epic made accessible to readers of all ages.
£3.95 *Paperback*
£5.95 *Hardback*

ST. PATRICK

George Otto Simms
The life of St. Patrick as he wrote it himself in his Confession, and the legends which have grown up around him.
Age group: 10-14 £6.95 *Hardback*

ALAS IN BLUNDERLAND

Peter Gunning
A whacky play based on legends and just about everything else, with director's notes and suggestions for production.
Age group: 6-12 (to act out) £4.95 *Paperback*

WILDLIFE AT RISK BOOKS 1 &2

Nature and craft books
Elizabeth Sides
Come face to face with endangered animals in this wildlife and craftwork series.
Age group: 6-10 £2.95 (each) *Paperback*

MOON CRADLE

Lullabies and Dandling Songs from Ireland with Old Childhood Favourites
Pat Donlon and Maddy Glas
A book of rhymes and songs of early childhood in both Irish and English with music.
Paperback £5.95

TOMMY – THE THEATRE CAT

Maureen Potter
A charming tale of backstage theatre life by this well-known entertainer.
Age group: 6-9 £3.95 *Paperback*

THE BOYNE VALLEY BOOK AND TAPE OF IRISH LEGENDS

More than an hour of the very best stories
£6.95 (*including tape*)

Busy Fingers – Art and Craft Series

1 SPRING
2 SUMMER
3 AUTUMN / HALLOWEEN
4 CHRISTMAS / WINTER

Sean C. O'Leary
A popular collection of simple and attractive things to make throughout the year.
Age group: 7-11 £1.95(each) *Paperback*

O'Brien Junior Biography Library

1 WOLFE TONE
2 W.B. YEATS
3 GRANUAILE
4 BOB GELDOF
5 SWIFT
6 MARKIEVICZ

Mary Moriarty and Catherine Sweeney
Major world figures in simple accessible language. Beautifully illustrated.
£3.95 (each) *Paperback*

*Send for our full colour catalogue
for more information*

THE O'BRIEN PRESS
20 Victoria Road, Dublin 6.
Tel: 979598 Fax: 979274